How to Write a Bestselling Fantasy Romance

From Myth to Manuscript: Building Your Fantasy Romance Universe

Just Bae

Contents

Introduction

Welcome to the enchanting world of fantasy romance, a genre where magic meets heart, and every story is an adventure of love and mystical quests. As an expert and best-selling author within this captivating genre, I've journeyed through countless worlds, crafting tales where dragons soar, and love transcends the boundaries of time and space. Fantasy romance isn't just about escapism; it's a celebration of imagination, a testament to the power of love in the face of darkness, and a genre that speaks to the heart of what it means to dream.

Fantasy romance combines the best of two worlds: the intricate world-building and epic scope of fantasy with the emotional depth and central focus on relationships found in romance. This fusion creates a unique space for storytelling, where authors can explore themes of destiny, power, sacrifice, and the magic of love itself. Characters in these stories often face not just external threats like dark wizards or ancient curses, but also the internal struggles of the heart, making their journeys deeply personal and universally relatable.

The genre's roots are as ancient as storytelling itself, with tales of mythical beings and mortal loves found in the folklore and myths of cultures worldwide. Yet, fantasy romance as we know it today has evolved significantly, influenced by shifts in society's understanding of love, power, and heroism. From the fairy tales of old to the complex narratives of today's bestsellers, the genre offers a rich tapestry of stories that resonate with readers of all ages.

Understanding the market and audience for fantasy romance is crucial for any author venturing into this realm. The genre's readers are diverse, seeking different experiences from their reading. Some may yearn for the thrill of adventure in fantastical lands, while others might seek the comfort of love's triumph over adversity. Yet, at the heart of every reader's quest is the desire for stories that captivate, inspire, and ultimately, transport them to worlds where anything is possible, and love is the greatest magic of all.

In recent years, the fantasy romance genre has seen a surge in popularity, driven by a growing appetite for stories that blend the escapist allure of fantasy with the emotional satisfaction of romance. This rise is reflected in the success of books like A Court of Thorns and Roses by Sarah J. Maas and Crescent City series, which have not only dominated bestseller lists but also sparked vibrant online communities of fans who dissect every detail of these richly imagined worlds and their romantic entanglements.

As we embark on this journey through the magic of fantasy romance, remember that at the core of every story lies the heart's power to overcome even the most formidable challenges. Whether you're a novice writer dreaming of penning your first novel or an experienced author seeking to delve deeper into the intricacies of the genre, the following chapters will guide you through the essentials of crafting compelling fantasy romance tales. From building enchanting worlds to creating characters that readers will fall in love with, the adventure begins here, in the realm where magic and romance intertwine seamlessly. Let's begin this journey together, and may your path be filled with wonder, danger, and, above all, love that defies all odds.

Chapter 1

What is Fantasy Romance

Fantasy romance is a genre that marries the escapism of fantasy with the emotional journey of romance. It transports readers to imagined realms where the laws of nature are often bent by magic and where the central plot revolves around the development of a romantic relationship against this enchanting backdrop. These narratives not only explore the boundless possibilities of the fantastic but also delve deeply into the intricacies of human (and sometimes non-human) relationships.

The defining feature of fantasy romance is its dual focus. The fantasy aspect is characterized by speculative fiction elements: magical powers, mythical creatures, and imagined worlds. Authors build intricate universes, complete with their own histories, languages, and cultures. The setting might be a medieval-inspired kingdom, a society where magic is hidden within the modern world, or even a completely alien environment with its own set of rules.

Parallel to the fantastical setting is the romance plot. Unlike in traditional fantasy, where romantic elements might play a supporting role, in fantasy romance, the development of the romantic relationship is front and center. The genre hinges on the emotional and often passionate connection between characters, with the love story undergoing various trials, tribulations, and triumphs. The romantic arc is given as much detail and depth as the world-building, ensuring that the readers are as invested in the relationship as they are in the lore of the world.

Fantasy romance embraces a variety of romantic themes, from the trope of star-crossed lovers to fated mates bound by destiny. Conflicts often arise not only from external magical or political struggles but also from personal and emotional obstacles. The protagonists might have to navigate not only a world of danger and intrigue but also their own fears, insecurities, and the vulnerability that comes with love.

The genre often includes subgenres, each with its own distinct flavors. High fantasy romance occurs in entirely fictional worlds, often in medieval or feudal settings. Urban fantasy romance is set in contemporary, real-world urban settings where magic and the supernatural exist secretly. Paranormal romance, a closely related cousin, typically involves supernatural creatures such as vampires, were-wolves, and ghosts in romantic relationships with humans or each other.

Diversity in fantasy romance has grown, with stories now encompassing a wide range of cultures, ethnicities, and sexual orientations. This inclusivity allows for a broader exploration of love and magic, resonating with a wider audience. Books like *Children of Blood and Bone* by Tomi Adeyemi and *The House in the Cerulean Sea* by TJ Klune celebrate this diversity, offering fresh perspectives within the genre.

The emotional stakes in fantasy romance are high, with the power of love often portrayed as a force that can overcome the greatest challenges. This is where the romance aspect elevates the fantasy, providing a human element to the grandeur and spectacle of the fantastical world. The genre promises not just an escape but an emotional odyssey that can be both exhilarating and heart-rending.

Fantasy romances have led to the flourishing of fan-driven content, such as fan fiction, art, and online discussions, which extend the life of the story beyond the page. The engagement between readers and writers in the fantasy romance community fosters a sense of belonging and shared ownership of the worlds and relationships that authors create.

As fantasy romance continues to evolve, it pushes the boundaries of both fantasy and romance. It is a genre unafraid to mix the whimsical with the profound, the magical with the mundane. Its narratives can be a refuge from reality and a mirror reflecting our deepest emotions and struggles. The genre speaks to the timeless human need for stories that inspire and move us and tales of love that are as boundless as our imaginations.

Fantasy romances captivate by celebrating the universal quest for connection and belonging in settings that ignite the imagination. It is a genre that promises readers an escape into the fantastic and a return to the essential truths of the human heart. Through the interplay of magic and emotion, fantasy romance affirms that love, in all its forms, is the truest adventure of all.

Chapter 2

The Evolution of Fantasy Romance

The origins of fantasy romance is steeped in the ancient traditions of folklore and myth, realms where the fantastical narratives of gods, mortals, and mythical beasts are often interwoven with the universal themes of love and desire. This rich tapestry of storytelling passed down through generations, serves as the bedrock upon which the fantasy romance genre is built. The enduring appeal of these tales lies in their ability to transport readers to worlds where the boundaries between the real and the imagined blur and where the pursuit of love transcends the ordinary constraints of existence.

Among the most influential precursors to the modern fantasy romance genre are the Arthurian legends. These medieval tales, with their intricate blend of chivalry, magic, and courtly love, not only captivated the imaginations of their contemporaneous audiences but have continued to inspire storytellers and readers alike for centuries. The legends of King Arthur, Guinevere, Lancelot, and the Knights of the Round Table highlight the complexities of love and honor, set against a backdrop of enchantment and heroic quests. The *Arthurian* tales underscore the genre's foundational belief in the transformative power of love, even amidst the trials of betrayal, jealousy, and warfare.

This early integration of romantic elements within fantastical narratives laid the groundwork for the genre's evolution. By marrying the extraordinary aspects of fantasy— such as magical spells, mythical creatures, and epic battles for justice or power—with the deeply human experiences of love, longing, and sacrifice, these stories created a blueprint for what would become fantasy romance. The genre thrives on the tension and harmony between these elements, exploring how love can both challenge and be challenged by the fantastical circumstances surrounding it.

The influence of folklore and myth on fantasy romance extends beyond the Arthurian legends to encompass a wide array of cultural traditions. From the Norse sagas, with their gods and giants entangled in fates both grand and personal, to the rich tapestry of Eastern mythology, where spirits and humans form bonds that defy the laws of nature, these stories contribute to the genre's depth and diversity. They provide a wellspring of motifs, archetypes, and narrative structures that modern fantasy romance authors draw upon to craft their own unique tales. These influences underscore the genre's ability to bridge different cultures and eras, showcasing the universal resonance of love intertwined with the fantastical.

* * *

After the Arthurian period, the historical evolution of fantasy romance traversed through the Renaissance and into the Enlightenment, where the genre began to shape itself more distinctly. Renaissance literature, such as the works of Edmund Spenser, particularly *The Faerie Queene,* presented allegorical narratives that combined elements of magic and chivalry with romantic undertones—this period cultivated an appetite for high romance set against a backdrop of elaborate, otherworldly landscapes, setting the stage for the more intricate world-building that would become a hallmark of fantasy romance.

In the 19th century, the gothic novel emerged as a significant influence on fantasy romance. Works like *Jane Eyre* by Charlotte Brontë, while not fantasy in the modern sense, wove together romance and the supernatural, hinting at the allure of mystery and the otherworldly in romantic contexts. Meanwhile, fairy tales collected by the Brothers Grimm and the romantic fantasies of George MacDonald introduced a direct link between the magical and the romantic, capturing imaginations with tales of heroic quests and love's transformative power.

The Victorian era saw an explosion of fantasy literature with romantic elements. Writers like William Morris and Lord Dunsany created works that laid the groundwork for modern high fantasy, incorporating medieval settings and chivalric romance that directly inspired later authors. At the same time, the pre-Raphaelite movement in art, which often took inspiration from these literary works, visually solidified the connection between fantasy and romance with its lush, dreamlike depictions of mythological and medieval subjects.

Entering the 20th century, the two World Wars and the period between them saw a shift in literary interests. Still, fantasy romance persisted through the works of authors like E.R. Eddison, whose novel *The Worm Ouroboros* combined heroic fantasy with courtly and romantic tradition. However, after the Second World War, fantasy romance began to take a more recognizable shape with the rise of modern fantasy literature. Tolkien's *The Lord of the Rings*, while primarily a high fantasy, contains subtle threads of romance, notably in the stories of *Aragorn* and *Arwen*, as well as *Eowyn* and *Faramir*, which would inspire future fantasy romance narratives.

The latter half of the 20th century saw fantasy romance emerge as a distinct genre, particularly with the rise of the paperback and the growth of genre fiction. Authors like Anne McCaffrey blended science fiction, fantasy, and romance in her *Dragonriders of Pern* series, and Mercedes Lackey introduced *Valdemar*, a world where love, whether it was romantic, platonic, or familial, often played a central role in her characters' stories. The fantasy romance genre began to flourish, with romance taking a central place in the plot and not just as a subplot to the fantasy narrative.

The 1980s and 90s marked a pivotal moment with the burgeoning popularity of paranormal romance and urban fantasy. Laurell K. Hamilton's Anita Blake: *Vampire Hunter* series and Charlaine Harris's *The Southern Vampire Mysteries* introduced a darker, more modern take on fantasy romance, mixing elements of mystery, horror, and eroticism. This period also saw the rise of magical realism, with authors like Isabel Allende and Alice Hoffman weaving romance through narratives that treated the supernatural as part of everyday life.

The turn of the millennium heralded a new era for fantasy romance with the advent of young adult (YA) fiction's explosive growth. Works like *Twilight* by Stephenie Meyer not only dominated bestseller lists but also introduced fantasy romance to a new generation. This trend continued with titles like Cassandra Clare's *The Mortal Instruments* series and Sarah J. Maas's *Throne of Glass* series, which combined rich fantasy worlds with complex romantic plots, appealing to both young adults and adult readers alike.

Today, fantasy romance stands as a genre that has fully come into its own, embracing the digital age with the rise of ebooks and online fan communities. Authors like Holly Black with *The Cruel Prince* and Tomi Adeyemi with *Children of Blood and Bone* continue to expand the genre's horizons, exploring diverse cultures and character backgrounds while intertwining romance with fantastical storytelling. The genre's adaptability and enduring appeal reflect a narrative tradition that values the power of love amidst the boundless possibilities of the fantastic.

Chapter 3

Your Targeting Audiences

Understanding the target audience for fantasy romance is essential for crafting stories that resonate and sell. This genre, rich with the allure of the fantastical and the intimate thrills of romance, attracts a surprisingly wide and varied readership. Its primary demographic has traditionally skewed towards women, particularly in the adult category, who often look for complex characters and emotional depth intertwined with the escapism of fantasy worlds. However, the misconception that fantasy romance is solely the domain of women is fading as the genre sees increasing interest from male readers, drawn to the elaborate world-building and the dynamic narrative arcs that challenge traditional gender roles within the scope of romantic fiction.

Young adult (YA) fantasy romance has carved out a significant niche in the market, appealing to teenagers and young adults with its themes of discovery, first love, and identity. Titles like *A Court of Thorns and Roses* by Sarah J. Maas have bridged the gap between teen and adult fiction, attracting older readers with their sophisticated themes and younger ones with their vibrant storytelling and relatable characters. The success of such series underscores the cross-generational appeal of fantasy romance, indicating a diverse age range among its audience.

The genre's appeal to an adolescent demographic doesn't stop with the young adult market. New Adult (NA) fantasy romance, targeting readers in their early twenties to mid-thirties, has grown in popularity. This subgenre addresses the transitional life phase between adolescence and full-fledged adulthood, with protagonists facing challenges related to independence, early career struggles, and mature relationships. Books like *Throne of Glass*, also by Maas, explore these themes, often with a more explicit approach to romance and character conflicts than is typically found in YA fiction.

Cultural diversity within the readership of fantasy romance has broadened the genre's horizons. Readers from various ethnic and cultural backgrounds seek stories reflecting their experiences and identities. The genre has responded with an increasing presence of multicultural and interracial romances set against the tapestry of fantasy worlds. Stories such as *Children of Blood and Bone* by Tomi Adeyemi resonate with readers looking for non-Western mythologies and characters with whom they can culturally identify.

Regarding content preferences, the fantasy romance audience tends to favor certain tropes and story mechanics. The 'enemies to lovers' arc is perennially popular, providing a dramatic tension that evolves into a passionate romance. Likewise, 'friends to lovers' and 'forbidden love' scenarios are recurring motifs that draw readers with their promise of emotional complexity and eventual romantic fulfillment. The trope of 'fated mates' in paranormal subgenres, as found in the *Seraph Black* series by Jane Washington, speaks to the allure of destiny and the idea of a love that is both inevitable and transformative.

The fantasy romance audience also displays a preference for strong, well-developed characters. Readers often seek out heroines who are not just passive recipients of affection but active agents in their own stories. They prefer heroes who are multi-dimensional and who respect the agency and strength of their partners. The interaction between such characters, such as those in *Radiance* by Grace Draven, must showcase growth, mutual respect, and equality, reflecting modern sensibilities and progressive values in relationships.

This audience values immersive world-building that doesn't overshadow the romantic plot. They look for settings that are integral to the characters' development and to the evolution of the romance itself. Settings should offer a blend of the familiar and the exotic, providing a stage upon which the drama of the romance can unfold. In books like *The Night Circus* by Erin Morgenstern, the world itself is almost a character, with its enchanting presence influencing the romance at the heart of the story.

The readership of fantasy romance also enjoys variety in the subgenres it explores. From the regal and knightly themes of high fantasy romance to the gritty streets of urban fantasy romance, there's an appreciation for different flavors of escapism. Subgenres like steampunk romance, which combines historical elements with anachronistic technological features, as seen in *Kiss of Steel* by Bec McMaster, offer a refreshing deviation from the medieval-centric settings often found in traditional fantasy.

The digital age has transformed how readers engage with fantasy romance. Online platforms have fostered vibrant communities where fans discuss their favorite books, share fan fiction, and interact directly with authors. This digital engagement has given rise to a feedback loop that shapes the genre, with reader preferences increasingly influencing the types of stories being written. The community's role in the evolution of fantasy romance cannot be overstated; authors and publishers alike pay close attention to the discussions and trends that emerge from online fan bases.

Chapter 4

What Niche, What Trope?

Fantasy romance, with its myriad of subgenres and themes, offers an extensive range of niches and tropes that cater to a variety of tastes and preferences. Each niche provides a unique spin on the genre, while tropes offer familiar narrative devices readers enjoy and expect.

One prominent niche within fantasy romance is high fantasy romance, which typically takes place in completely imaginary worlds with their own set of rules, races, and histories. High fantasy romance often includes epic quests and the romance may be interwoven with the fate of the kingdoms or worlds. Tropes popular in this niche include the "noble hero" or "warrior princess," who fall in love while battling a greater evil, exemplified in series like *The Wheel of Time* by Robert Jordan, where romantic subplots enrich a complex, multifaceted narrative.

Another popular niche is the paranormal romance, which often overlaps with urban fantasy romance. This subgenre brings supernatural elements into a modern setting, incorporating creatures like vampires, werewolves, and witches. A common trope here is the "forbidden love" between a supernatural being and a human, such as in the *Twilight* series by Stephenie Meyer, which explores the tumultuous romance between a vampire and a human girl.

Urban fantasy romance focuses on supernatural elements in urban settings, with protagonists often involved in investigating paranormal incidents or conflicts. Tropes such as "hidden worlds" within our own and "mates in the midst of chaos" are prevalent, as seen in *The Dresden Files* by Jim Butcher, where the protagonist wizard often deals with romantic relationships amid supernatural investigations.

The "fated mates" trope is a mainstay in fantasy romance, particularly in subgenres involving shifters or otherworldly creatures. This trope plays on the idea of destined love and the irresistible pull between two characters, which can add a sense of inevitability and passion to the romance. *The Black Dagger Brotherhood* series by J.R. Ward showcases this trope within its vampire-centric narrative.

Time travel romance is a niche that merges the concept of time travel with love stories. A classic trope in this category is "love across time," where characters from different eras fall in love, such as in *Outlander* by Diana Gabaldon. The trope explores the challenges and allure of a love that transcends time itself.

In the fairy tale retelling niche, authors re-imagine classic fairy tales with a romantic twist, often adding depth and new perspectives to well-known stories. Tropes such as "the beast redeemed by love" or "the hidden prince/princess" are common, offering fresh takes on familiar tales. An example is *Beauty* by Robin McKinley, which provides a deeper, more nuanced exploration of the Beauty and the Beast story.

Reverse harem is a niche that has gained popularity, where a protagonist has several love interests and does not have to choose just one by the story's end. The trope of "one true heroine, multiple loves" caters to fantasies of polyamorous relationships or non-monogamy, often set against a backdrop of fantasy world intrigue.

The "enemies to lovers" trope is a fan favorite in fantasy romance, where two characters start as adversaries and develop a romantic relationship throughout the story. This dynamic allows for intense emotional development and dramatic tension, as seen in *The Cruel Prince* by Holly Black.

The "magical bond" trope is frequently found in fantasy romance, involving a connection between characters that is both magical and unbreakable, dictating a deep and often complicated relationship. This is depicted in series like *The*

Witchlands by Susan Dennard, where the bond affects both the plot and the romance arc.

The "chosen one" trope, while a staple in fantasy literature, also finds its place in fantasy romance. In these narratives, a character destined for greatness finds love along their journey, which can humanize the "chosen one" and add layers of personal conflict. The trope is often used to intertwine personal growth with the development of romantic feelings, as seen in *Graceling* by Kristin Cashore.

Let's look at the tropes in detail:

Fated Mates: The trope of fated mates is especially prevalent in fantasy romance, playing upon the idea of predestined love that is often linked to supernatural or magical forces. In these narratives, characters are irresistibly drawn together by an inexplicable connection that suggests they are destined for one another. This can manifest as an innate magical bond or a prophecy intertwining their fates. The allure of this trope lies in its exploration of destiny versus choice and the intense emotional and physical connection it creates between characters. Series like *The Night Huntress* by Jeaniene Frost exemplify this, weaving a powerful narrative of passion and destiny.

The fated mates trope resonates with readers because it speaks to the fantasy of finding a perfect counterpart, someone who is meant for them in every sense. It creates a compelling narrative tension as the characters often struggle against this preordained pull due to personal conflicts or external forces. Yet, the inevitability of their union provides a satisfying culmination to the romantic arc, often acting as a catalyst for character growth and plot development.

Enemies to Lovers: In the enemies to lovers trope, characters initially clash with clashing ideologies, competing objectives, or simply personal dislike. However, as the story unfolds, animosity turns to understanding, respect, and ultimately romance. This trope allows for a rich exploration of character depth and development, as protagonists must reconcile their preconceptions with the evolving reality of their adversary-turned-partner. Notable examples include *The Wrath & the Dawn* by Renée Ahdieh, where a vengeful heroine falls for the very king she intended to kill.

The tension inherent in the enemies-to-lovers trope is its main draw, providing a roller coaster of emotions as characters transition from conflict to passionate love. This dynamic sets the stage for powerful scenes of confrontation and reconciliation, often forcing characters to confront their flaws and prejudices. The trope is celebrated for its ability to build a strong foundation for the relationship as the characters earn each other's trust and respect, giving their eventual romantic union a sense of hard-won victory.

Forbidden Love: Forbidden love stories are rife with drama and tension, as the characters involved engage in a relationship that is somehow prohibited—be it by family, society, or law. This creates a framework for high stakes and the thrill of secrecy, as seen in *Star-Touched Queen* by Roshani Chokshi, where celestial interference and cursed fates hinder the protagonists' union. The taboo nature of the romance often amplifies the emotional intensity and the sense of urgency within the narrative.

Readers are drawn to the forbidden love trope because it embodies the struggle against external forces for the sake of love. It's a testament to the enduring power of the human heart. The inherent risk in these relationships makes every moment more poignant, every touch more significant, and the triumph of love all the more exhilarating. Forbidden love stories reaffirm the notion that love knows no bounds and can flourish even in the most inhospitable environments.

Magical Bond: The magical bond trope features characters linked by a mystical connection that transcends mere attraction. This bond often has implications for both the plot and the relationship dynamics, as it can compel the characters to stay close or understand each other's thoughts and emotions, as illustrated in *A Court of Thorns and Roses* by Sarah J. Maas. The bond may be a blessing or a curse, creating an intricate dance of intimacy and autonomy.

This trope appeals to readers because it adds an element of the extraordinary to the romance. The magical bond can act as a metaphor for the deep connection and understanding we seek in relationships. It also presents characters with unique challenges to overcome, ensuring the romantic tension remains high throughout the story. The magical bond, in its various forms, adds a layer of complexity to the characters' interactions and decisions, enriching both the fantasy and romantic elements of the narrative.

Chosen One: The chosen one trope often places a character at the center of prophecy or destiny, imbued with the power or responsibility to effect great change. When combined with romance, this trope explores how such a grand role impacts personal relationships and the dynamics of love. Characters must balance the weight of their destiny with their desires, leading to poignant drama and conflict. Laini Taylor's *Daughter of Smoke & Bone* series provides a stunning example of a protagonist grappling with a world-altering fate while navigating a profound romantic connection.

The chosen one trope in romance allows readers to explore the themes of sacrifice, duty, and the price of greatness in conjunction with the pursuit of love. It raises questions about free will and the individual's role in shaping their destiny. The interplay between a predestined path and the unpredictability of love creates a compelling, thought-provoking, and emotionally charged juxtaposition. The romance that blooms in the shadow of such immense responsibility is often all the more poignant for the obstacles it must overcome.

Star-Crossed Lovers: The trope of star-crossed lovers depicts a romance that seems doomed from the start due to external forces, such as feuding families, disparate social statuses, or even cosmic influences. This theme, which traces its origins back to works like Shakespeare's Romeo and Juliet, is a powerful narrative engine in fantasy romance, driving stories where love must struggle against the odds. In *Stardust* by Neil Gaiman, for example, the lovers come from different worlds—literally—and must overcome not only personal but interdimensional obstacles to be together.

The appeal of the star-crossed lovers trope lies in the intense longing and desperation that permeate the relationship. Readers are drawn to the emotional depth that arises from the tension between a seemingly fated love and the insurmountable obstacles it faces. The trope promises a narrative filled with passion, sacrifice, and the questioning of destiny, which often leads to a bittersweet or hard-earned resolution, making the eventual triumph of love—if it comes—all the sweeter.

Beauty and the Beast: The 'Beauty and the Beast' trope, a timeless narrative of seeing beyond appearances and finding love, remains a beloved staple in fantasy romance. This trope usually involves a character who is cursed or has a monstrous appearance and a partner who comes to see the beauty within them. A classic iteration of this is found in *Beauty* by Robin McKinley. This direct retelling captures the essence of the trope while adding depth to the romance and the fantasy elements.

The *'Beauty and the Beast'* narrative resonates with readers because it speaks to the transformative power of love and acceptance. It suggests that empathy and kindness can unlock the redemptive potential within anyone, a deeply appealing concept. Moreover, it often involves a gradual and tender growth of affection that evolves into a deep, understanding love, which can be incredibly satisfying to follow. The trope usually explores themes of identity, self-worth, and the influence of societal expectations, making it as relevant today as ever.

Soulmates: The soulmates trope is centered on the concept of two characters being perfect matches for each other, often with a supernatural or predestined aspect to their connection. These soulmates are drawn together by forces greater than themselves, and their relationship is characterized by an intense bond that transcends physical attraction. In *The Time Traveler's Wife* by Audrey Niffenegger, the connection between the protagonists defies time constraints, underscoring the depth of the soulmate trope in a unique twist.

Readers are attracted to the soulmates trope for its idealistic portrayal of love as an unparalleled and inescapable force. It offers a narrative certainty that, despite any adversities, the characters are meant to be together, providing a comforting and reassuring storyline. The exploration of such a deep connection often allows for a rich exploration of the characters' psyches, as they are usually mirrors of each other's souls, designed to complete and understand one another on an almost cosmic level.

The Quest: In many fantasy romance stories, the quest's trope serves as the narrative's driving force. It's a journey undertaken by the protagonists, fraught with danger, adventure, and an array of challenges that test their skills, beliefs, and bonds. The quest often serves as a catalyst for romance, forcing the characters into close proximity and shared experiences that draw them together. *The Hobbit* by J.R.R. Tolkien, while not primarily a romance, includes elements of this trope that have influenced subsequent fantasy romance narratives.

The quest trope is beloved because it combines action and adventure with character development and romantic tension. As the characters face external challenges, they are also navigating the burgeoning or deepening of their romantic feelings. The shared adversity of the quest can lead to moments of vulnerability and honesty, accelerating the emotional intimacy between the characters. The journey motif also allows for expansive world-building and the introduction of varied settings that keep the narrative fresh and engaging.

Guardian/Ward: The guardian/ward trope involves one character charged with protecting another, often leading to a mix of romantic tension and a sense of duty. This dynamic can create complex power imbalances that the story must address and resolve. An example of this can be found in *The Queen's Thief* series by Megan Whalen Turner, where the intricate interplay between the guardian and the protected individual evolves into a nuanced relationship.

This trope captivates readers by offering a blend of tenderness and tension. The protector's instinct to care for their ward can evolve naturally into deeper feelings, while the ward's reliance on the guardian can lead to a close, almost symbiotic bond. The trope explores themes of trust, loyalty, and the transition from dependence to equality. It offers fertile ground for exploring the balance of power in relationships and how love can emerge from a foundation of mutual respect and admiration.

Hidden Legacy: The hidden legacy trope features characters who discover they have a secret heritage or unknown powers that suddenly thrust them into new and often perilous circumstances. This revelation is typically a turning point in the narrative and can be the catalyst for romantic developments, as seen in *The Grisha Trilogy* by Leigh Bardugo. The character's newfound abilities or status changes the dynamics of their relationships, often attracting allies and adversaries, including potential romantic interests.

Audiences enjoy the hidden legacy trope for the sense of wonder and the character's journey of self-discovery it brings. There is a vicarious thrill in watching an ordinary individual grapple with extraordinary new realities, and romance often adds a grounding human element to this metamorphosis. The trope also allows for dramatic reveals and twists that can keep readers invested in both the plot and the evolving romantic arc.

Opposites Attract: In the opposites attract trope, two characters with contrasting personalities, beliefs, or backgrounds find themselves drawn to each other, often overcoming initial friction or misunderstandings. This contrast can create a dynamic tension that is both comedic and endearing, as seen in *The Princess Bride* by William Goldman, where the sweet and dreamy Buttercup falls for the cynical and world-weary Westley. Their differences ultimately complement each other, leading to a romance as captivating as the unexpected.

The appeal of the opposites attract trope lies in the journey from discord to harmony. Readers enjoy the banter and sparks that fly as the characters challenge and change each other, often leading to personal growth and deepening their relationship. This trope plays on the idea that love can bridge the gap between disparate worlds, offering a message of hope and unity that is particularly resonant in fantasy romance, where differences can be as vast as different species or worlds.

The Reluctant Hero/Heroine: The reluctant hero or heroine is a character who is thrust into an adventure or role of significance they initially resist but ultimately embrace, often becoming a key figure in the narrative. This trope is compelling because it mirrors the common human experience of hesitancy in the face of change or greatness. In *The Summoning* by Kelley Armstrong, the protagonist is an unwilling necromancer who must come to terms with her powers and, through this journey, encounters potential romantic interests that support or challenge her emerging identity.

This trope resonates with readers due to its relatability and the character development it naturally entails. The reluctant hero's or heroine's journey from denial to acceptance is often paralleled by a romantic subplot where love acts as a motivator or reward. Their internal struggle can create a rich emotional landscape for a romance to blossom, with their partner often serving as a catalyst for their transformation. The romantic interest may also have a complementary reluctance or readiness that adds depth and complexity to the relationship.

Secret Heir/Heiress: In the secret heir or heiress trope, a character discovers they are the hidden descendants of a powerful lineage or kingdom, often placing them at the center of political intrigue and danger. This revelation can disrupt the character's life and relationships, adding layers of complexity to their romantic entanglements. A prime example is *Red Queen* by Victoria Aveyard, where the protagonist's latent abilities reveal her to be part of a powerful and contested heritage.

The secret heir or heiress trope is a favorite among readers for its mix of escapism and wish fulfillment. The transformation from obscurity to prominence makes for a compelling narrative arc enriched by romance, as the character's partner must adapt to the new reality alongside them. The trope often explores themes of identity, belonging, and the burden of responsibility, providing a dramatic backdrop for the evolution of the romantic relationship.

Arranged Marriage: The arranged marriage trope involves characters compelled into a relationship by external forces, such as political alliances, peace treaties, or familial obligations. This starting point sets the stage for a complex emotional journey as the characters navigate their duties and growing feelings for each other. In *Radiance* by Grace Draven, the protagonists are from different species and must overcome significant cultural and physical differences to find common ground and affection.

The trope allows readers to explore the development of love and respect in a constrained setting, often leading to deep and meaningful connections. The arranged marriage scenario forces proximity and can accelerate intimacy, turning what could have been a mere alliance into a profound romance. It also introduces a tension between societal expectations and personal desires, providing a rich ground for characters to challenge traditional norms and assert their agency.

The Protector: A common fantasy romance trope is the protector: a character often tasked with guarding another, leading to a close and complex relationship. The dynamic is ripe with potential for conflict and romance, as the protector must balance their duty with their growing personal attachment. In *The Queen of Attolia* by Megan Whalen Turner, the queen's personal guard becomes integral to the story, with his unwavering loyalty evolving into a deeper, more intimate bond.

Readers are drawn to the protector trope for the inherent tension it creates. It's a relationship built on trust and the constant interplay between strength and vulnerability. As the protector and their charge navigate dangers and adversaries, they come to rely on each other, often developing a mutual respect that serves as the foundation for romantic feelings. The trope also allows for a display of heroism and self-sacrifice, qualities particularly appealing in the context of a romance.

The Curse: The curse trope is a mainstay of fantasy romance, involving a character who suffers from a magical affliction that can only be broken by a specific act, often related to love. This setup creates a sense of urgency and a poignant quest for redemption, as seen in *A Curse So Dark* *and Lonely* by Brigid Kemmerer, which reimagines the *Beauty and the Beast* narrative with a modern twist. The cursed character's plight often elicits sympathy and a rooting interest from the reader, enhancing the emotional stakes of the romance.

The draw of the curse trope is its embodiment of the theme that love is a transformative and healing force. The journey to break the curse provides a narrative framework for the characters to develop a deep and sacrificial love, often involving trials that test their commitment and fortitude. The curse can also serve as a metaphor for personal demons or societal barriers, adding layers of meaning to the romantic narrative and emphasizing the power of love to overcome even the most formidable obstacles.

Lost Heir/Heiress: The lost heir or heiress trope involves a character, often with a mysterious past, who is revealed as the missing scion of a powerful family or kingdom. This discovery usually propels the story forward, entangling the protagonist in a web of intrigue and romance. The trope is exemplified in books like *The Kiss of Deception* by Mary E. Pearson, where the protagonist's hidden identity is central to both the plot and the romantic tension that ensues.

This trope resonates with readers due to the allure of hidden identities and the unraveling of secrets. The lost heir or heiress must often navigate a new world of power and expectation, which can create compelling internal and external conflicts, especially when intertwined with romantic elements. Discovering their true identity can lead to reevaluating their relationships, often resulting in an exploration of authenticity and trust within the romantic arc.

Cross-Cultural Romance: In the cross-cultural romance trope, characters from vastly different backgrounds, races, or even species find love with one another. This theme explores the challenges and beauties of bridging cultural divides, often against broader societal tensions or prejudices. An example of this trope is found in *The Bird and the Sword* by Amy Harmon, where characters from opposing kingdoms and with differing magical abilities must navigate their forbidden love amidst war and prophecy.

This trope resonates deeply with readers for its exploration of themes such as acceptance, diversity, and the universality of love. It reflects a broader societal conversation about inclusivity and overcoming barriers to understanding and unity. In fantasy romance, cross-cultural relationships are enriched by the genre's ability to exaggerate differences— through magical abilities or fantastical races—thereby amplifying the narrative's exploration of partnership, compromise, and the celebration of diversity within the tapestry of love.

The Reluctant Hero/Heroine: The reluctant hero or heroine trope features a protagonist who is unexpectedly called to embark on a quest or take on a role of significance, often while dealing with their own personal issues or reluctance to accept their destiny. This journey is not only one of external adventure but also of internal growth, which becomes intertwined with a developing romantic subplot. For example, in *Poison Study* by Maria V. Snyder, the protagonist starts as a condemned prisoner and grows into a powerful figure in a complex political and magical landscape, all while navigating the waters of unexpected love.

Readers are drawn to the reluctant hero/heroine trope because it showcases character development and personal growth in the face of adversity. The character's initial hesitation or refusal to embrace their destiny makes their eventual acceptance and success all the more rewarding. As these characters grow, they often find love—not as a reward for their heroism but as a natural progression of their journey toward understanding themselves and their place in the world. The romantic elements in these stories highlight the vulnerability and strength that come from love, reinforcing the idea that personal transformation and love can go hand in hand.

Magic as a Barrier to Love: In some fantasy romance stories, magic acts as a barrier to the romantic relationship. This can take many forms, from curses that prevent characters from being together to differences in magical ability that create social or personal obstacles. An example of this is *A Curse So Dark and Lonely* by Brigid Kemmerer, a retelling of *Beauty and the Beast*, where a curse traps the prince in a cycle of reliving the autumn of his eighteenth year until he can find true love.

This trope explores the complexities of love in the face of seemingly insurmountable challenges. It adds a layer of tension and urgency to the romance, as the characters must not only navigate their feelings but also seek solutions to the magical barriers that separate them. Readers are captivated by the creativity with which characters address these obstacles, and the theme underscores the power of love to overcome even the most daunting barriers. The trope speaks to the resilience of the human spirit and the lengths to which people will go for love, making the eventual triumph over magical adversity a testament to the enduring power of connection and affection.

Reincarnation and Past Lives: The trope of reincarnation and past lives introduces a fascinating dynamic into fantasy romance, where characters may be drawn together or torn apart by the echoes of their past incarnations. This can create a narrative where discovering past connections deepens the current romance or introduces conflict that must be resolved. An enchanting example is found in *The Night Circus* by Erin Morgenstern, where the intertwined destinies of the characters across time add a profound depth to their relationship.

This theme captivates readers with the notion that love can transcend time and that souls can find each other again against the odds. It adds a mystical dimension to the romance, imbuing the relationship with a sense of fate and destiny that is larger than life. Exploring reincarnation and past lives also allows for rich storytelling that can span different eras and settings, providing a lush backdrop for the romantic plot. It raises questions about identity, destiny, and the nature of love itself, making for a deeply engaging and often poignant reading experience.

Arranged Marriage: The arranged marriage trope explores the dynamics of characters brought together through political, familial, or societal arrangements rather than mutual attraction. In the realm of fantasy romance, this setup provides fertile ground for exploring themes of duty versus desire and the growth of love and understanding over time. A classic example within fantasy settings is *Radiance* by Grace Draven, where two characters from different species are united in marriage to cement an alliance between their peoples. Initially, their relationship is one of convenience and mutual respect, but it gradually evolves into a deep, genuine love.

This trope resonates with readers because it reflects the complex journey from obligation to affection, highlighting the development of trust, respect, and, ultimately, love between the characters. It challenges the notion of "love at first sight" by proposing that love can be a slow burn, growing from shared experiences and overcoming prejudices. The arranged marriage scenario also allows for rich world-building, as the reasons behind the arrangement often tie into the setting's political, cultural, or magical elements, providing a backdrop that enriches the romance.

Secret Royalty: In fantasy romance, the secret royalty trope involves characters who are unaware of their royal heritage or who hide their identity for safety, political, or personal reasons. This trope adds layers of intrigue and complexity to the narrative, as the revelation of a character's true status can drastically change the dynamics of their romantic relationship. An example of this is found in *The Queen of the Tearling* by Erika Johansen, where the protagonist must navigate her hidden identity as well as the challenges and responsibilities it brings, all while encountering potential romantic interests.

The allure of the secret royalty trope lies in its exploration of identity, power, and the burden of responsibility. For readers, there's a thrilling tension in waiting for the moment when the character's true heritage is revealed and seeing how it affects their romantic relationship. It also allows for a deeper examination of character, as the protagonist often must reconcile their perceived identity with their true one. Additionally, this trope speaks to the fantasy of discovering one's own hidden greatness or importance, making the romantic journey even more compelling as it intertwines with a narrative of self-discovery and acceptance.

Forbidden Magic: Forbidden magic serves as a compelling trope in fantasy romance, where the use or existence of certain magical abilities is outlawed or feared. Characters involved in such romances often face persecution or have to hide their true powers, adding an element of danger and secrecy to their relationship. This is vividly portrayed in *Shadow and Bone* by Leigh Bardugo, where the protagonist discovers a rare magical ability that thrusts her into a world of intrigue and conflict, affecting her relationships.

This trope explores themes of persecution, secrecy, and the moral dilemmas associated with wielding great power. It heightens the stakes of the romance, as characters must navigate not only their feelings for each other but also the external pressures that threaten to tear them apart. Forbidden magic often serves as a metaphor for forbidden love, emphasizing the idea that societal norms or laws cannot constrain genuine connection. Readers are drawn to the tension and the thrill of clandestine meetings, as well as the hope that love will ultimately transcend the barriers imposed by a world that fears their power.

Protector and Protected: The dynamic of protector and protected is a common trope where one character is assigned or feels compelled to guard the other, often leading to a deepening of their relationship over time. This setup provides a clear power dynamic that can evolve as the protected character grows stronger or as the protector becomes vulnerable, allowing for a rich exploration of trust and dependence. In *Throne of Glass* by Sarah J. Maas, the skilled assassin protagonist becomes a protector in various capacities, navigating complex relationships and romantic tensions that challenge her solitary nature.

This trope appeals to readers because it often starts with a clear imbalance of power or ability, which evolves into mutual respect and dependence. The protector role can shift between characters, reflecting growth and change in their relationship. It also introduces a natural intimacy as the characters are thrown together by circumstance, relying on each other for survival. The evolution from protector and protected to partners in love and battle showcases a journey of mutual respect, trust, and, ultimately, equality that resonates with readers looking for a romance that grows out of shared experiences and challenges.

Chapter 5

Don't Forget to Merge Myth with Magic

Merging myth and magic with romance creates a unique narrative alchemy that captivates readers by intertwining the familiarity of mythological archetypes and the enchantment of magic with the universal appeal of romantic storytelling. This fusion allows authors to explore timeless themes of love, destiny, and heroism through a lens that is both other-worldly and deeply human. Myths, with their rich tapestry of gods, monsters, and heroes, provide a vast reservoir of motifs and archetypes from which fantasy romance writers can draw, offering a sense of depth and resonance to the narrative. When these elements are skillfully combined with the personal and emotional journey of romance, the story gains an epic dimension, elevating the stakes and intensifying the emotional impact.

Magic, both literal and metaphorical, amplifies the drama and complexity of romantic relationships in these narratives. It can act as a barrier, bond, or catalyst, transforming the mundane into the extraordinary and reflecting the characters' internal landscapes. The use of magic in romance can symbolize the inexplicable nature of love—the way it defies logic alters perceptions and changes individuals. In stories where characters wield magical powers or encounter magical beings, their romantic journey often mirrors their magical one, with both paths requiring self-discovery, acceptance, and the courage to embrace the unknown. This parallel draws readers deeper into the world of the story, engaging them on multiple levels.

Integrating myth into fantasy romance enriches the narrative with a layer of cultural and historical significance, grounding the fantastical elements in a shared human heritage. Myths from different cultures offer diverse perspectives on love, sacrifice, and power, allowing for a broad exploration of these themes. By reimagining mythological tales with a romantic focus, writers can challenge and reinterpret traditional narratives, giving voice to characters who might have been sidelined in the original myths. This revitalizes ancient stories for a modern audience and allows for a more inclusive and varied representation of love and heroism.

The romance in these stories often transcends the personal, affecting the world around the characters in profound ways.

In myths, love can be a force of creation or destruction, leading to the rise or fall of kingdoms and altering the course of destiny. This concept is expanded in fantasy romance, with the love between characters often acting as a key to resolving the larger magical or mythological conflicts. This elevates the romance from a simple interpersonal connection to a pivotal element of the plot, emphasizing the power of love as a transformative force.

Moreover, the setting in such narratives—whether a detailed recreation of a mythological world or an entirely new universe inspired by mythic elements—provides a rich backdrop for the romantic plot. The fantastical landscapes, populated with mythical creatures and governed by ancient magics, contribute to an atmosphere of wonder and danger. This setting intensifies the romantic relationship, as the characters must navigate their feelings for each other and the challenges of their environment. The otherworldliness of the setting serves to highlight the characters' emotional journey, making their love all the more poignant for its survival against such a backdrop.

Chapter 6

Finding your Niche

Finding your niche as a fantasy romance writer is crucial to defining your voice and attracting a dedicated readership. Your niche is where your passion meets the specific tastes and interests of a segment of readers within the broader fantasy romance genre. It's about honing in on the elements that excite you most—be it high fantasy settings, paranormal beings, or timeless tales of forbidden love—and using them to carve out a unique space for your stories.

Start by exploring the subgenres of fantasy romance to identify where your interests lie. Are you drawn to the intricate political and magical systems of high fantasy worlds? Or do you prefer the dark allure of paranormal romance, with its vampires, werewolves, and other supernatural creatures? Perhaps you're captivated by the idea of retelling classic fairy tales with a fresh, romantic twist. Each of these paths offers a distinct flavor of fantasy romance, and your affinity for one over the others can guide you toward your niche.

Consider the themes and tropes that resonate with you and how they can differentiate your work. Themes of destiny versus free will, the power of love to transcend barriers, or the transformational nature of love within a magical context might speak to you. Tropes like star-crossed lovers, fated mates, or enemies-to-lovers can be explored in new and inventive ways within your chosen subgenre. Your unique take on these elements can set your stories apart and attract readers who share your interests.

Reflect on the myths, legends, and folklore that inspire you. These stories are rich with archetypal characters and plots that have captivated human imagination for centuries. Drawing on such timeless material can lend depth and universality to your fantasy romance, anchoring it in the collective unconscious while allowing you to explore new narrative possibilities. Your niche might involve weaving these ancient narratives with original romantic plots, bridging the old and the new.

Pay attention to the settings that ignite your creativity. The world you build is the stage upon which your romantic drama unfolds, and its uniqueness can be a significant part of your appeal. Whether you're creating a lush, detailed fantasy world, a hidden magical society within our modern world, or a post-apocalyptic landscape with remnants of magic, the setting can play a crucial role in defining your niche. A vividly imagined world that complements and challenges your characters' romance can become as memorable as the love story itself.

Understand the importance of character development in finding your niche. Fantasy romance thrives on the strength of its characters—their struggles, their growth, and their relationships. Your ability to create compelling, multifaceted characters who navigate the challenges of your fantastical settings while experiencing profound emotional journeys can be a defining feature of your niche. Whether your protagonists are warriors, sorcerers, or ordinary people faced with extraordinary circumstances, their development is key to engaging your readers.

Explore the dynamics of romance in your storytelling. How you depict romantic relationships—be it slow-burn romances, love at first sight, or complex polyamorous dynamics—can help define your niche. Your approach to romance, including how you handle themes of consent, equality, and partnership, can set you apart and appeal to readers seeking specific types of romantic narratives.

Engage with the fantasy romance community to refine your understanding of your niche. Reader feedback, discussions with fellow writers, and reviews of similar works can offer invaluable insights into what resonates with audiences. This engagement can also reveal gaps in the market that your work could fill, helping you to refine your niche further.

Stay true to your voice and vision. While market trends can guide you, your niche should reflect your unique perspective and passion. Writing the stories you want to tell in a way only you can will attract readers who appreciate your authentic voice and the particular blend of fantasy and romance you offer.

Experiment with mixing genres to create something uniquely yours. Fantasy romance is a blend of genres, but within its broad umbrella, there's room to incorporate elements from science fiction, historical fiction, or even horror. Drawing on multiple genres allows you to create a niche that defies easy categorization, offering readers familiar tropes in unexpected contexts. A historical fantasy romance set in a meticulously researched Victorian London, infused with steampunk technology and a dash of Gothic horror, can offer a reading experience that stands out in the crowded marketplace.

Focus on character archetypes that intrigue you. Perhaps you have a penchant for writing about anti-heroes or trickster figures whose moral ambiguity adds depth to the romantic plot. Or maybe you're drawn to strong, independent heroines who defy societal expectations. By consistently writing characters who embody certain traits or archetypes, you can establish a niche that attracts readers who share your fascination. Characters like these, who break molds and challenge norms, can become a signature feature of your work, differentiating your fantasy romances from others.

Consider the type of world-building that excites you. Some authors find their niche in the intricacy of their worlds, crafting elaborate magic systems, rich historical backdrops, or detailed cultural customs. If you delight in creating worlds as complex and immersive as those found in epic fantasy but with a strong romantic core, this can become a defining aspect of your niche. Your ability to transport readers to these fully realized worlds, where romance blooms amidst magic and intrigue, can become a key draw.

Pay attention to pacing and structure in your stories. Your preference for fast-paced, plot-driven narratives versus slow, character-focused explorations can influence your niche. Some readers might be drawn to your work for its quick-moving plots that blend romance and fantasy action, while others might appreciate the slow burn of a romance that develops over the course of a deeply detailed fantasy saga. Your approach to pacing and how you balance plot with character development can set your stories apart.

Reflect on the kinds of conflicts and challenges you like to explore. The obstacles lovers face in fantasy romance vary widely, from external threats like wars and political intrigue to internal struggles such as secrets and personal growth.

Your niche might emerge from the specific types of conflict you find most compelling to write about, whether they're epic battles between good and evil or more intimate, psychological battles within a character's heart.

Stay informed about current trends and reader preferences within the fantasy romance genre, but don't be afraid to go against the grain. While knowing what readers enjoy is helpful, true innovation often comes from offering something new and unexpected. Your niche might lie in filling a gap you've identified in the market or merging trends in a way that hasn't been seen before.

Finally, be open to evolution. Your niche might shift as you grow as a writer and as reader tastes change. The fantasy romance genre is broad and varied, with plenty of room for exploration and innovation. Embracing change and being willing to explore new aspects of the genre can keep your writing fresh and exciting for you and your readers.

Finding your niche as a fantasy romance writer is a journey of exploration and self-discovery. By focusing on the aspects of the genre you love most and infusing your stories with your unique voice and perspective, you can carve out a space that satisfies your creative passion and resonates deeply with readers.

Chapter 7

Avoiding Clichés

Avoiding clichés, especially in fantasy romance, requires a keen awareness of genre conventions and a creative approach to storytelling. This genre, rich with possibility, often falls prey to overused tropes and predictable plotlines that can dull the impact of a narrative. To craft stories that feel fresh and engaging, writers must navigate these waters carefully, seeking innovative ways to tell their tales of magic and love.

One common cliché is the trope of the damsel in distress, where a female character is rendered powerless and waits to be rescued by a male hero. This trope can be subverted by creating female characters who are capable, complex, and active participants in their own stories. For example, in *The Bear and the Nightingale* by Katherine Arden, the protagonist, Vasya, defies the passive damsel role by embracing her power and fighting for her community. Writers can offer a more nuanced and empowering narrative by giving female characters agency and roles that defy traditional expectations.

The concept of 'love at first sight' is another cliché that permeates the genre, often reducing the development of a relationship to an instant connection that lacks depth. To avoid this, authors can gradually focus on building relationships, allowing characters to grow, challenge each other, and bond over shared experiences. In *Strange the Dreamer* by Laini Taylor, the relationship between Lazlo and Sarai develops through shared dreams and deep conversations, creating a connection that feels earned and genuine.

The chosen one narrative, where a single character is destined to save the world, can also become clichéd without careful handling. This trope can be refreshed by distributing the responsibility among a cast of characters, each contributing their unique skills towards a common goal, as seen in *Six of Crows* by Leigh Bardugo. This approach not only democratizes the concept of heroism but also allows for a richer exploration of teamwork and love in various forms.

Magical solutions to romantic obstacles can feel like a convenient deus ex machina, undermining the complexity of the characters' journey. Instead, magic can come with its own set of challenges and limitations, making the path to love more complicated and, therefore, more rewarding. In *A Darker Shade of Magic* by V.E. Schwab, magic complicates relationships and demands sacrifices, making the characters' choices and struggles more impactful.

The evil antagonist who opposes the lovers for the sake of conflict can be a reductive element in fantasy romance. A more nuanced approach involves antagonists with relatable motivations and backstories whose opposition arises from genuine beliefs or situations. *Serpent & Dove* by Shelby Mahurin presents an antagonist whose actions are deeply tied to personal loss and cultural beliefs, adding layers to the conflict.

Another cliché is the use of prophecy to drive the narrative, often dictating the course of the romance. Subverting this trope might involve characters who actively resist or misunderstand prophecy, leading to unexpected outcomes. In *The Raven Boys* by Maggie Stiefvater, the prophecy surrounding Blue's true love adds complexity to her relationships, challenging preconceived notions of destiny.

While compelling, the trope of forbidden love can become clichéd if the reasons for the prohibition lack depth or originality. Creating societies with unique cultural or magical reasons for forbidding certain relationships can add intrigue. For instance, in *Delirium by Lauren Oliver*, love is literally outlawed, providing a fresh take on the theme of forbidden romance.

Overuse of the alpha male archetype in romantic leads can also feel clichéd. Offering a range of romantic interests with diverse personalities, vulnerabilities, and strengths can appeal to a broader audience and reflect more realistic and respectful dynamics. *The Long Way to a Small, Angry Planet* by Becky Chambers showcases a variety of relationships that defy traditional archetypes, enriching the narrative tapestry.

In addition to challenging traditional tropes and clichés, fantasy romance writers can also focus on the depth of their world-building. Often, stories fall into the cliché of vaguely medieval European settings without much thought to the societal, cultural, or magical systems that govern them. By diversifying settings and drawing inspiration from a wide range of cultures and historical periods, authors can create vibrant, unique worlds that stand apart. For example, *The Golem and the Jinni* by Helene Wecker blends elements of Jewish and Syrian folklore, setting its magical romance in the immigrant communities of turn-of-the-century New York City, offering a fresh and compelling backdrop that enriches the narrative.

Another way to avoid clichés is by reimagining the role of magic in romantic relationships. Rather than magic being a mere plot device to bring lovers together or tear them apart, it can be used to explore deeper themes of identity, consent, and sacrifice. In *The Paper Magician* series by Charlie N. Holmberg, magic is intimately tied to the characters' emotions and growth, making their romantic development feel organic and integral to the plot. This approach ensures that magic and romance are woven together in a way that enhances both elements, providing a richer and more satisfying story.

The cliché of the lone hero or heroine can also be subverted by emphasizing community and found family. In many fantasy romances, the protagonists' journey is often solitary, focusing solely on their development and romantic interests. However, incorporating a strong sense of community and support networks can add depth to the narrative and offer new dynamics for exploring romantic relationships. *Foundryside* by Robert Jackson Bennett introduces a cast of characters whose relationships with one another provide a foundation for growth and change, including romantic developments, highlighting the importance of community in personal and romantic evolution.

Subverting the trope of instant love or attraction can add realism and depth to fantasy romance. Instead of characters falling in love at first sight, exploring slow-building relationships that develop from friendship, respect, or even initial dislike can make the romance more believable and engaging. *The Bone Season* series by Samantha Shannon gradually develops the central romance over time, allowing for character development and a buildup of mutual understanding and respect, culminating in a more meaningful connection.

Inverting the power dynamics often seen in fantasy romance can also provide a fresh perspective. Traditionally, narratives might lean towards powerful magical beings falling for seemingly less significant mortals. Flipping this dynamic, where the seemingly ordinary character has much to offer and teach the magical partner, can challenge conventional power structures and offer a narrative of mutual growth and respect. *Strange Grace* by Tessa Gratton explores complex relationships within a magical framework, focusing on equality and the subversion of traditional roles, which enriches the story's romantic and fantastical elements.

Addressing personal agency and independence themes within the romantic plot is another way to move beyond clichés. Rather than romance being the sole defining feature of a character's arc, stories can highlight characters' quests for personal growth, ambition, and self-discovery, with romance as a complementary, enriching aspect of their journey. *Circe* by Madeline Miller, for example, focuses on the titular character's path to self-empowerment and identity, with romantic elements that underscore, rather than overshadow, her development.

Finally, embracing complexity in character relationships can help avoid the cliché of the perfect, unchallenged romance. Acknowledging and exploring conflicts, misunderstandings, and growth within relationships can make for a more compelling and realistic narrative. *The Priory of the Orange Tree* by Samantha Shannon delves into the complexities of political intrigue, personal duty, and the challenging path to trust and understanding between characters, presenting a multifaceted view of love in a richly built world.

By thoughtfully challenging and reimagining clichés, fantasy romance writers can craft stories that captivate and resonate with readers on deeper levels. The key lies in innovative storytelling, rich character development, and the courage to explore new territories in the genre, ensuring that each love story told is as unique and magical as the worlds they inhabit.

Chapter 8

Be Original

Originality in romantic and fantastical elements is the cornerstone of fantasy romance literature. The fresh infusion of ideas and perspectives keeps readers engaged, turning pages eagerly to discover new worlds, magic systems, and the dynamics of relationships that defy their expectations. In a genre where familiar tropes often provide the framework for storytelling, originality isn't just about avoiding clichés; it's about elevating the narrative to explore uncharted territories of the heart and imagination. Originality ensures a story stands out in a crowded market, offering readers something they haven't seen before and imbuing the tale with a unique voice that resonates long after the final page is turned.

In fantasy, originality in the magical system and world-building can turn a simple love story into an epic saga that captivates the imagination. When magic operates under unique laws or is used in novel ways to influence the plot and the characters' relationships, it adds intrigue and complexity to the narrative. Consider the intricate magic of Brandon Sanderson's *Cosmere* universe, where distinct magical systems form the backbone of various series. Applying such creativity to fantasy romance, where the magic directly impacts the romantic relationship, can add depth and originality to the story, allowing the romance to unfold in unexpected ways that challenge both the characters and their perceptions of love and power.

The originality of the fantastical setting is equally important. A vividly imagined world with unique cultures, histories, and conflicts provides a rich backdrop for the romantic plot. It's not just about crafting a setting where magical elements exist but how these elements affect society, traditions, and interpersonal relationships within the story. A novel like *The City of Brass* by S.A. Chakraborty, with its rich Middle Eastern setting filled with djinn and ancient magic, showcases how originality in world-building can create a mesmerizing stage for romance to bloom, intertwining with political intrigue and personal growth.

Furthermore, originality in depicting romance—how love is expressed, challenged, and celebrated—can elevate a fantasy romance novel. Moving beyond the traditional narratives of instant attraction or love triangles to explore themes of partnership, sacrifice, and consent within the context of a magical world makes the romance feel more natural and relevant. Stories that portray healthy, equitable relationships or navigate the complexities of love in innovative ways resonate with readers seeking escapism and emotional truth. *This Is How You Lose the Time War* by Amal El-Mohtar and Max Gladstone exemplifies this, presenting a love story through letters across time and war, showcasing originality in romantic and fantastical elements.

Originality also lies in the diversity of characters and relationships. Fantasy romance thrives when it mirrors the real world's complexity, including a range of experiences, orientations, and identities. Crafting characters who defy genre stereotypes—not just in their roles as heroes or heroines but in their desires, flaws, and journeys—makes for a more inclusive and engaging reading experience. The exploration of LGBTQ+ relationships, polyamory, or culturally diverse partnerships within the context of a fantasy setting, as seen in *The House in the Cerulean Sea* by TJ Klune, not only broadens the genre's appeal but also enriches its narrative depth.

The integration of unique romantic and fantastical elements requires a delicate balance. The fantastical aspects must enhance the romance without overshadowing it, and the love story should feel integral to the plot, driving the characters' decisions and the story's outcome. Achieving this harmony makes the novel more than just a series of events;

it becomes a compelling narrative where magic and romance are inextricably linked, each amplifying the other.

Moreover, originality fosters a deeper connection between the reader and the story. When readers encounter a novel that defies their expectations, it engages their imagination and emotions more fully, inviting them into a partnership with the author to explore the story's unique world and the complexities of its characters' relationships. This engagement transforms a simple read into a memorable experience that readers are eager to return to and recommend to others.

The importance of originality in romantic and fantastical elements cannot be overstated. It's the spark that ignites the imagination, the thread that weaves through the narrative to connect the reader, character, and author in a shared experience of discovery and emotion. For fantasy romance writers, embracing originality is not just a challenge but an opportunity—to enchant, innovate, and contribute to the evolving tapestry of the genre.

Chapter 9

Building your Fantasy World

Building a world of fantasy that captivates readers requires a meticulous balance between imagination and consistency, especially when it comes to the rules governing magic and fantastical elements. The creation of a magical system isn't merely about deciding what is possible within your universe but also about defining the limitations and costs of using such power. This framework not only adds depth and realism to your world but also provides a fertile ground for conflict, character development, and plot progression. A well-thought-out magical system, as seen in *Mistborn* by Brandon Sanderson, where metals are consumed to grant powers, showcases how rules can enhance the story's tension and the characters' challenges.

The process of world-building within these rules begins with a clear understanding of how magic influences society, culture, and daily life in your fantasy world. Consider whether magic is a common gift or a rare talent, and how its distribution among the population shapes social hierarchies and power dynamics. In *The Name of the Wind* by Patrick Rothfuss, magic is academically studied and practiced, integrating it into the society's structure and economy, which provides a backdrop for personal and political conflicts within the story.

Integrating fantasy elements seamlessly into your world also involves creating a history that feels lived-in and real. This history should reflect the evolution of magic and its impact on the world's development, including past conflicts, discoveries, and pivotal figures in the lore. Such a backdrop not only enriches the narrative but also offers opportunities for plot developments rooted in historical events or ancient secrets, as seen in the complex backstory of *A Song of Ice and Fire* by George R.R. Martin.

The geography and environment of your fantasy world can also be profoundly affected by its magical rules. Landscapes might be shaped by magical forces, with certain areas being imbued with magical properties that affect the flora, fauna, and climate. This environmental aspect of world-building not only adds visual richness and diversity but also challenges characters to adapt to or harness these conditions, as explored in the vivid settings *of The Stormlight Archive*, also by Brandon Sanderson.

Cultural diversity within your world should reflect the variety of ways different societies understand, use, and regulate magic. This can lead to a rich tapestry of beliefs, rituals, and conflicts, offering a multi-faceted view of magic that enhances the story's depth and complexity. *The Poppy War* by R.F. Kuang presents magic through the lens of different cultural traditions and historical contexts, enriching the narrative and providing a nuanced exploration of power.

The rules for magic in your world should also include clear limitations and consequences. This not only prevents characters from becoming omnipotent, which can deflate tension and stakes but also introduces moral and ethical dilemmas. Deciding the cost of magic—whether it's a physical toll on the user, a depletion of natural resources, or a societal taboo—adds layers to the narrative, as characters must weigh their actions against these consequences, a theme effectively utilized in *The Magicians* by Lev Grossman.

Language and terminology related to magic and fantastical elements should be thoughtfully developed to enhance the immersive experience. Creating specific terms for magical practices, creatures, and artifacts can lend authenticity to your world and help readers differentiate between various aspects of your fantasy universe. The unique vocabulary *of Harry Potter* by J.K. Rowling, for example, has become iconic, enriching the world's texture and engaging readers.

The interaction between magic and technology in your world can offer an interesting dimension to explore. In settings where magic coexists with or substitutes for technology, consider how this affects societal development, warfare, and daily life. *Perdido Street Station* by China Miéville blends magic with steampunk technology, creating a unique world where the two forces interplay in complex and often conflict-ridden ways.

Religious and philosophical beliefs about magic can add depth to your world-building, influencing everything from governance and law to personal identity and conflict. These beliefs can serve as a source of conflict, provide motivations for characters, and add a layer of complexity to the narrative. In *The Fifth Season* by N.K. Jemisin, the societal understanding and control of magical abilities are central to the plot, reflecting deeper themes of oppression, identity, and resistance.

Finally, consider the narrative possibilities of evolving or hidden aspects of your magical system. Introducing discoveries, innovations, or lost knowledge about magic can drive your plot forward, offering opportunities for surprise and wonder both for your characters and your readers. The gradual unveiling of the deeper rules of magic in *The Wheel of Time* series by Robert Jordan serves as a compelling narrative device that keeps readers engaged throughout the saga.

By meticulously crafting the rules for magic and fantasy elements within your world, you create a framework that supports and enriches your narrative. This careful balance between the boundless possibilities of magic and the grounded realities of its limitations and consequences ensures that your fantasy world captivates readers with its originality, depth, and coherence.

Chapter 10

Creating a Setting that Complements the Romance Arc

Complimenting the romance arc in fantasy literature involves more than just providing a backdrop for the characters' journey—it means constructing a world that actively enhances and reflects the development of the romantic relationship. A well-crafted setting can mirror the characters' emotional landscape, offer obstacles that test their bond, and provide a space where their love can flourish against all odds. For instance, in *Outlander* by Diana Gabaldon, the lush and tumultuous Highlands of Scotland serve not just as a setting but as an integral component of Claire and Jamie's romance, with its dangers and beauties mirroring the complexities of their relationship.

The physical environment can be a metaphor for the relationship at different stages. A stormy, rugged coastline might reflect turmoil and conflict, while a serene, hidden valley offers a haven for intimacy and growth. In Juliet Marillier's *Daughter of the Forest*, the dense, mysterious forest serves as a critical element of the plot. It mirrors the protagonist's isolation and her path to save those she loves. In this way, the setting becomes a silent narrator of the romantic journey, with its shifts paralleling those in the relationship.

Historical or mythical elements embedded in the setting can also play a significant role in the romance arc. By drawing on legends or historical events specific to the setting, you can add depth to the romance, tying the characters' love story to the fate of their world. In *A Song of Ice and Fire* by George R.R. Martin, the rich history of Westeros, with its tales of ancient loves and betrayals, sets a precedent for the complex relationships that unfold, suggesting that the past continually echoes in the present.

Magic within the setting can directly influence the romance arc as a catalyst for the relationship and a source of conflict. Whether it's a curse that needs to be broken through true love's kiss or magical laws that forbid relationships between certain classes of mystical beings, these elements can add tension and stakes to the romance. In *The Night Circus* by Erin Morgenstern, the enchanting, mysterious circus is a setting and a manifestation of the magical competition between the protagonists, binding them together in a complex blend of rivalry and love.

Cultural and societal norms within your fantasy world can provide a rich tapestry against which the romance unfolds. How societies view relationships, marriage, and duty can create external pressures that the protagonists must navigate. This is evident in *The Wrath & the Dawn* by Renée Ahdieh, where Shahrzad marries the caliph not out of love but as part of a plan for revenge. The setting's cultural expectations and political intrigue significantly impact their relationship's evolution, highlighting how societal context can shape personal dynamics.

Your setting can offer unique opportunities for the characters to grow closer or be torn apart. Hidden groves, ancient ruins, and bustling city markets can all serve as stages for key moments in the romance. These locations can facilitate intimacy through shared secrets or discoveries or bring conflict through dangers and societal judgment. For instance, the floating islands and constantly shifting landscapes in Strange the Dreamer by Laini Taylor provide a dreamlike quality to the setting, echoing the surreal and hopeful nature of the protagonists' love while presenting literal heights and falls that mirror the ups and downs of their relationship.

By thoughtfully integrating the setting with the romance arc, writers can enhance the emotional resonance of their story, making the world an active participant in the unfolding love story. This approach ensures that the setting is not just a backdrop but a crucial element that enriches and complicates the romance, offering readers a fully immersive and emotionally engaging experience.

Chapter 11

Romantic Relationships through Culture and Society

In fantasy literature, the culture and society in which a story is set play pivotal roles in shaping the contours and dynamics of romantic relationships. These elements provide a framework of norms, values, and expectations that characters must navigate, enriching the narrative with layers of complexity and realism. Through the lens of fantasy, authors have the unique opportunity to explore how cultural and societal constructs influence personal relationships, offering insights that resonate with the real-world experiences of their readers.

One way culture and society impact romantic relationships in fantasy stories is through the concept of arranged marriages or alliances. Such arrangements often serve as a narrative device to explore themes of duty versus desire, where characters are torn between their obligations to their family or society and their personal feelings. This is vividly portrayed in *The Bone Season* series by Samantha Shannon, where hierarchical structures and clashing cultures dictate the terms of relationships, challenging the protagonists to find their paths to love amidst political and social turmoil. These stories delve into the emotional and ethical dilemmas faced by characters, highlighting the tension between individual autonomy and societal expectations.

Another aspect is the societal attitudes toward gender roles and sexuality, which can significantly influence the development of romantic relationships. Fantasy settings often reimagine or exaggerate these attitudes, creating worlds where gender and sexuality are fluid and diverse or, conversely, where they are rigidly defined and policed. This allows authors to critique or affirm certain societal norms, as seen in *The Priory of the Orange Tree* by Samantha Shannon, where same-sex relationships are normalized in some cultures but taboo in others. Through the lens of fantasy, authors can challenge contemporary notions of gender and sexuality, allowing readers to envision alternative models of identity and relationship dynamics.

The intersection of class, caste, or racial divisions within fantasy societies also profoundly impacts romantic relationships. Such divisions can create barriers to love, mirroring real-world issues of prejudice and inequality. In *Children of Blood and Bone* by Tomi Adeyemi, the tensions between the oppressed maji and the ruling kosidán form the backdrop for the characters' relationships, underscoring how societal divides based on power and privilege can shape personal connections. By navigating these divides, characters often challenge the status quo, and their love becomes a symbol of resistance and hope for a more equitable world.

Religious and philosophical beliefs within fantasy cultures further influence romantic relationships, often dictating what is considered morally acceptable or forbidden. Depending on the cultural context, these beliefs can imbue romance with a sense of sacrality or profanity. In *The Kushiel's Legacy* series by Jacqueline Carey, the protagonist's divine mandate to experience love and pain as worship challenges the societal norms of her time, weaving a complex tapestry of religion, politics, and romance. Through such narratives, fantasy literature can explore the profound impact of spiritual and ethical convictions on love and relationships, reflecting on the diversity of belief systems in our own world.

Cultural rituals and celebrations related to love and partnership in fantasy societies offer rich narrative opportunities to explore the customs that bind people together or keep them apart. These rituals, whether elaborate courtships, magical bonding ceremonies, or trials of compatibility, add depth to the world-building and provide milestones in the characters' romantic journeys. *A Court of Thorns and Roses* by Sarah J. Maas exemplifies this with rituals that intertwine magic, love, and fate, showcasing how cultural practices can challenge and cement relationships.

Societal conflicts, such as wars, political upheaval, or clashes between magical factions, can drastically affect romantic relationships. In such tumultuous contexts, love can be a source of strength and refuge or a vulnerability to be exploited. *The Queen of Tearling* by Erika Johansen explores how the protagonist's ascending to the throne impacts her personal desires and relationships, set against the backdrop of political intrigue and war. This highlights how external pressures can forge bonds of solidarity and love or, conversely, tear them apart.

Through the intricate interplay of culture and society, fantasy literature illuminates the myriad ways external forces shape the course of love, offering readers escapism and a mirror to reflect on their own world's complexities and contradictions.

Chapter 12

Creating Memorable Characters

Creating memorable hero and heroine archetypes in fantasy romance involves blending traditional archetypal characteristics with unique, individual traits that make your characters stand out. In a genre rich with possibilities, the challenge lies in crafting protagonists who resonate with readers through their fantastical roles and their deeply human emotions and struggles. A well-designed hero or heroine can become the heart of the story, driving the plot forward and engaging the reader on an emotional journey of love, conflict, and growth.

The first step in creating memorable protagonists is to consider the classic archetypes that have captivated audiences for centuries—the warrior, the mage, the rogue, or the monarch, among others. These archetypes offer a familiar foundation, giving readers an immediate sense of the character's role in their world. However, the key to making these characters memorable is adding depth and complexity that transcend their roles. For instance, a warrior heroine might not only excel in physical combat but also grapple with the moral implications of her actions, as seen in *Graceling* by Kristin Cashore, where Katsa's journey involves reconciling her lethal skills with her desire for peace and autonomy.

Another aspect of crafting memorable heroes and heroines is to infuse them with flaws and vulnerabilities. Characters who are too perfect can feel distant and unrelatable, while those who struggle, make mistakes, and grow are more compelling and human. These flaws can be internal, such as self-doubt or fear, or external, such as societal expectations or physical limitations. A mage with unparalleled power might struggle with control or fear of their abilities, adding layers to their character and creating opportunities for growth and development within the romance arc.

Diversity in character backgrounds and experiences enriches the tapestry of fantasy romance. Heroes and heroines who represent a wide range of cultures, identities, and experiences bring fresh perspectives to the genre. Incorporating characters with diverse backgrounds reflects the richness of the real world and allows for the exploration of unique conflicts, relationships, and magical systems. In *The Wrath & the Dawn* by Renée Ahdieh, Shahrzad's cultural heritage and personal vendetta against the caliph serve as driving forces in her story, enhancing the depth of her character and the complexity of her romance with Khalid.

The dynamics of power play a significant role in shaping memorable fantasy romance protagonists. Characters can wield power in various forms—magical, political, or personal—and how they navigate this power significantly impacts their relationships and personal growth. A heroine who rises to lead a rebellion, like *Mare Barrow in Red Queen* by Victoria Aveyard, must balance her newfound power with her vulnerabilities and desires, providing a compelling narrative of leadership intertwined with romance.

Inner conflicts and desires are crucial in defining hero and heroine archetypes. Characters driven by strong, personal motivations—whether protecting their loved ones, seeking redemption, or challenging the status quo—resonate more deeply with readers. These motivations can conflict with their romantic desires, creating tension and depth in the narrative. For example, in *A Darker Shade of Magic* by V.E. Schwab, Lila Bard's thirst for adventure and freedom clashes with her growing bond with Kell, making their relationship all the more intriguing.

The relationship between the hero and heroine (or hero/hero, heroine/heroine) can also define their archetypes. Their romance should challenge and transform them, pushing them beyond their limits and compelling them to confront their deepest fears and desires. The dynamic between the protagonists, whether based on mutual respect, fiery conflict, or a blend of both, should evolve naturally, reflecting their individual journeys and the obstacles they face together.

Finally, integrating the protagonists' romantic journey with the broader world and plot of your fantasy romance is essential. Their relationship should feel like a natural extension of the narrative, with their love influencing and being influenced by their world's magical and political machinations. In *Crescent City: House of Earth and Blood* by Sarah J. Maas, the personal growth of the protagonists and the evolution of their relationship are intricately linked with the unfolding mysteries and conflicts of the larger story.

Creating memorable hero and heroine archetypes in fantasy romance is about balancing the familiar with the innovative, grounding the fantastical in the deeply human, and weaving the threads of romance and adventure into a cohesive, compelling narrative. By focusing on depth, growth, and the unique interplay between characters and their world, authors can craft protagonists who linger in the minds and hearts of readers long after the story ends.

Chapter 13

Make your Romantic Relationships Believable

A believable romantic relationship within the fantastical context of a fantasy romance novel requires a nuanced understanding of both the genre's conventions and the universal truths of love and human connection. The allure of fantasy romance lies in its ability to transport readers to worlds of wonder and magic. Yet, the core of its appeal remains the emotional authenticity of its central relationship. To achieve this, authors must weave the fantastical elements of their world seamlessly with the development of the romance, ensuring that the love story resonates with readers on a deeply personal level.

One of the first steps in crafting a believable romantic relationship is to establish strong, multidimensional characters who can navigate the wonders and perils of their world while also experiencing the universal joys and challenges of love. These characters should have distinct personalities, backgrounds, and motivations that make them compelling individuals and set the stage for a dynamic and evolving relationship. Their interactions should reflect a gradual understanding and appreciation of each other's qualities, flaws, and desires. In *The Night Circus* by Erin Morgenstern, the romance between Celia and Marco is built on mutual admiration and deep, albeit competitive, understanding, making their love feel inevitable and true despite the novel's enchanting and surreal setting.

Another crucial aspect is the integration of the fantastical elements with the romantic plot. Magic, mythical creatures, and otherworldly landscapes should do more than just provide a backdrop for the romance; they should actively influence the relationship's development. Whether it's a curse that needs breaking, a magical bond that draws the lovers together, or a quest that tests their commitment, these elements can add depth and complexity to the romance. In *A Court of Thorns and Roses* by Sarah J. Maas, the magical laws and curses directly impact the protagonists' relationship, intertwining their love story with the fate of their world.

Conflict and obstacles are essential in developing a believable romantic relationship, allowing characters to grow individually and as a couple. In a fantasy setting, these challenges can range from external threats, such as warring factions or evil forces, to internal struggles, such as fear of rejection or the burden of secrets. How characters navigate these obstacles, relying on each other's strengths and accepting each other's weaknesses, reinforces the authenticity of their bond. *Shadow and Bone* by Leigh Bardugo effectively uses the conflict between darkness and light, literally and metaphorically, to test and ultimately strengthen the bond between Alina and Mal.

Communication is pivotal in building a realistic romance, even in a world of magic and mystery. Honest dialogue, shared vulnerabilities, and moments of understanding bridge the gap between the fantastical and the relatable, allowing readers to connect with the characters' emotional journey. Effective communication doesn't mean the absence of misunderstandings or secrets; instead, it's about how characters resolve these issues, demonstrating growth and commitment. *The Wrath & the Dawn* by Renée Ahdieh showcases how communication, or the lack thereof, can drive the story's tension while providing a pathway to deeper intimacy.

The pacing of the relationship is another important consideration. A romance that unfolds too quickly can feel superficial, while one that drags on without significant development may lose the reader's interest. Balancing attraction with genuine connection and initial conflict with gradual resolution helps to create a believable and engaging romance. For instance, the slow-burn romance in Uprooted by Naomi Novik allows for a natural progression from antagonism to affection, grounded in shared experiences and mutual respect.

Lastly, the conclusion of a romantic arc in a fantastical context should offer both resolution and a sense of continuity. While the climax may involve epic battles or magical showdowns, the resolution of the romance should feel grounded in the characters' journey and growth. Whether it's a happily-ever-after or a more nuanced acknowledgment of love's complexities, the ending should reflect the authenticity of the relationship within the bounds of the world you've created. *The Queen of Nothing* by Holly Black concludes with a resolution that honors the tumultuous yet undeniable bond between Jude and Cardan, satisfying readers with a conclusion that feels both earned and true to the fantastical world they inhabit.

In crafting believable romantic relationships in fantasy romance, the key is to blend the extraordinary with the universal, ensuring that the heart of the story—its emotional truth—remains relatable and resonant, no matter how fantastical the setting.

Chapter 14

Antagonists and Obstacles

In fantasy romance, antagonists and obstacles serve as the crucible through which the strength and depth of the central relationship are tested and ultimately affirmed. These narrative elements are not mere hurdles but are integral to the plot, enriching the story with tension, conflict, and the potential for character growth. A well-crafted antagonist or obstacle can elevate the narrative, transforming a simple love story into a saga of resilience, sacrifice, and triumph.

Antagonists often embody the darker aspects of the world the author has created. They can be tyrannical rulers, evil sorcerers, or vengeful gods whose goals are opposed to those of the protagonists. However, the most memorable antagonists are those with nuanced motivations and complex personalities who offer a glimpse into the potential darkness within us all. In Serpent & Dove by Shelby

Mahurin, the antagonist's earnest desire to eradicate witch-craft stems from a place of personal loss and societal indoctrination, providing a multifaceted view of villainy that challenges the protagonists and the reader alike.

Obstacles in fantasy romance are not limited to external conflicts but often include internal struggles that characters must overcome to be together. These can range from secrets and past traumas to differences in social status or race. Such obstacles add layers to the relationship, forcing characters to confront their adversaries and their own fears and prejudices. In The Bridge Kingdom by Danielle L. Jensen, the protagonists must navigate a web of political intrigue and personal betrayals, where trust becomes both a precious commodity and a potential downfall.

The setting can act as an antagonist, presenting natural and supernatural challenges that test the protagonists' resolve and the strength of their bond. A world plagued by perpetual winter, a kingdom on the brink of war, or a landscape imbued with deadly magic can all serve as formidable obstacles. In The Wrath & the Dawn by Renée Ahdieh, the cursed land provides a backdrop against which the romance unfolds, with its dangers mirroring the tumultuous nature of the protagonists' relationship.

Societal norms and expectations often play the role of antagonist in fantasy romance, imposing constraints on the characters' love. Whether it's a taboo against fraternizing with the enemy or prohibitions based on class or magic, these societal obstacles create a tension between duty and desire. An Ember in the Ashes by Sabaa Tahir explores this theme, depicting a world where love is a risk and a defiance of the oppressive order, making the protagonists' relationship a beacon of hope and rebellion.

Using curses or prophecies as obstacles introduces an element of fate into the romance, challenging the characters to defy destiny for the sake of love. This trope can add a mythic dimension to the story, as in A Curse So Dark and Lonely by Brigid Kemmerer, where the protagonists must navigate the complexities of a curse that entwines their lives in unexpected ways. The struggle against such a preordained path emphasizes the power of choice and the courage to forge one's destiny.

Magical barriers or enchantments can also serve as obstacles, with characters forced to seek out solutions or make sacrifices to be together. These challenges often require a deep exploration of the magical world the author has created, showcasing the protagonists' ingenuity and determination. In *Strange the Dreamer* by Laini Taylor, the city of Weep is shadowed by mysteries and enchantments that separate the lovers, making their quest to be together as much about solving the city's woes as it is about overcoming their personal barriers.

The theme of forbidden love is a powerful obstacle in fantasy romance, where characters must challenge the taboos of their world to be together. This can stem from differences in race, species, or magical affiliation, as seen in *Blood and Ash* by Jennifer L. Armentrout, where the protagonists' love defies the strictures of their society, setting the stage for conflict and change. The allure of forbidden love lies in its testament to the idea that love can transcend boundaries, offering a narrative of defiance and liberation.

Rivalries or competitions can also act as obstacles, pitting the protagonists against each other or against a common enemy. This dynamic can fuel the narrative with tension and excitement, as in *The Hunger Games* by Suzanne Collins; though not strictly a fantasy romance, the competitive setting provides a framework for the evolving relationship between Katniss and Peeta, highlighting themes of survival, alliance, and love under duress.

The consequences of magic or power misuse offer another layer of obstacles in fantasy romance. Characters might grapple with the fallout of their actions or the actions of those around them as the misuse of magical abilities threatens their world's balance. *The Magicians* by Lev Grossman delves into the darker side of magic and its personal costs, weaving a tale where love and magic are both wondrous and perilously fraught.

In crafting these antagonists and obstacles, the key is to ensure they enrich the story, providing avenues for character development and opportunities for the protagonists' love to prove its mettle. By navigating these challenges, the characters demonstrate their worthiness of the love they fight for, making their eventual union all the more satisfying. The best fantasy romance stories are those where the journey to love is as compelling and intricate as the world in which it unfolds, with every antagonist faced and obstacle overcome adding to the depth and resonance of the central relationship.

Chapter 15

Structuring your Plot

Structuring a plot that equally balances fantasy and romance is a meticulous endeavor, requiring a deep understanding of both genres to weave them seamlessly into a cohesive narrative. This balance ensures that neither element overshadows the other, but rather, they complement and enhance one another, creating a richer and more engaging story. To achieve this, authors must first establish a clear understanding of the stakes involved in both the fantasy and the romantic elements of their story. The fantasy world's conflicts, whether they involve battling dark forces, unraveling ancient curses, or securing a fragile peace, must intersect with the romantic plot in a way that each propels the other forward. For instance, in *Daughter of Smoke and* Bone by Laini Taylor, the epic battle between angels and demons is intricately linked to the protagonists' past and future romance, making their love story pivotal to the resolution of the broader conflict.

The key to balancing fantasy and romance begins with character development. Protagonists should be crafted with care, ensuring they have stakes in the story's fantastical and romantic aspects. Their personal growth, challenges, and triumphs should be influenced by the magical world they inhabit, as well as by their romantic relationships. Characters must navigate their world's complexities— political intrigue, magical laws, or ancient prophecies—while also exploring the depths of their emotions and relationships. This dual journey makes characters more relatable and multifaceted and ties the romance and fantasy elements together naturally. In *A Court of Thorns and Roses* by Sarah J. Maas, Feyre's evolution from a mere mortal to a powerful figure in a magical court is deeply entwined with her romantic entanglements, demonstrating how love and power can intersect.

Plot pacing is critical in maintaining the balance between fantasy and romance. The narrative should allow moments of high-stakes fantasy action, such as battles or quests, to coexist with quieter, more intimate moments where the romance can blossom. This pacing ensures the story maintains momentum while providing the depth needed for the romantic relationship to develop believably. Authors might employ alternating plot points focusing on the fantasy and romance elements, ensuring that each has room to breathe and impact the story. In *The Night Circus* by Erin Morgenstern, the pacing deftly oscillates between the enchanting competitions of the circus and the deepening love story between Celia and Marco, creating a mesmerizing tale that captivates readers with both its imaginative breadth and emotional depth.

Incorporating themes that resonate across fantasy and romance can also unify the plot. Themes such as sacrifice, destiny, betrayal, and redemption can have profound implications in the fantastical setting and the romantic relationship. By weaving these themes throughout the narrative, authors can create a cohesive and resonant plot, with each aspect of the story reinforcing the other. In *The Wrath & the Dawn* by Renée Ahdieh, the theme of vengeance transitions into one of understanding and love, linking the fantastical element of a cursed prince with the deeply personal journey of a young woman set on revenge.

The setting of the fantasy romance is another tool authors can use to balance the plot. A well-realized setting integral to both the fantasy elements and the romantic plot can serve as a connecting thread between the two. The environment can influence the characters' actions, shape the obstacles they face, and set the stage for key romantic developments. Whether it's a bustling city where magic lurks in the shadows or a desolate landscape that tests their survival and commitment, the setting should catalyze the fantasy and romance plotlines. In *Strange the Dreamer* by Laini Taylor, the city of Weep is not just a backdrop but a character in its own right whose mysteries and history are central to the conflict and the romance.

Finally, the story's resolution should bring both the fantasy and romance arcs to a satisfying conclusion, addressing the central conflicts and answering the key questions raised throughout the narrative. This doesn't necessarily mean a traditional "happily ever after," but rather a conclusion that feels true to the world and characters the author has created. The end should reflect the journey the characters have undertaken, the battles they've fought, and the love they've forged, underscoring the inseparable bond between the fantastical and romantic elements of the story. In *The Queen of Nothing* by Holly Black, the culmination of Jude and Cardan's tumultuous relationship and the political intrigue of Elfhame come together in a climax that resolves both the personal and political tensions in a way that feels both earned and inevitable.

Balancing fantasy and romance requires a delicate touch, ensuring that both elements are interwoven throughout the plot, enriching and propelling each other forward. When done successfully, the result is a story that offers the best of both worlds: the escape and wonder of fantasy, paired with the emotional depth and resonance of romance.

* * *

In fantasy romance, the key plot points that define the genre blend the enchanting allure of fantasy with the emotional journey of romance, creating narratives that captivate with both their imaginative scope and their heartfelt connections. One of the first unique plot points often involves the protagonists' destined meeting or fateful encounter. Unlike traditional meet-cutes, these encounters are imbued with magic or prophecy, setting the tone for a relationship that is as much about navigating the complexities of love as it is about fulfilling destiny. For instance, in *A Court of Thorns and Roses* by Sarah J. Maas, Feyre's life-changing encounter with Tamlin is steeped in curses and prophecies, intertwining their fates in ways that deeply affect both the fantastical and romantic arcs of the story.

Another pivotal plot point unique to fantasy romance is the revelation of a secret world or hidden identity, which catalyzes both the adventure and the development of the romance. This moment of revelation propels the protagonists into the heart of the fantasy narrative and challenges their preconceptions about each other and the world around them, deepening their connection. In *Crescent City: House of Earth and Blood* by Sarah J. Maas, the discovery of hidden truths about the city and its inhabitants forces the protagonists to confront their secrets and lies, weaving together elements of mystery, fantasy, and romance.

Introducing a common enemy or overarching threat is a crucial plot point that unites the protagonists in a shared cause, further binding their destinies together. This antagonist, often a figure of great power or malice, represents not just a threat to the world but also a direct challenge to the protagonists' burgeoning relationship. The struggle against this enemy provides numerous opportunities for the protagonists to demonstrate their loyalty, bravery, and love for each other, as seen in *Shadow and Bone* by Leigh Bardugo, where Alina and Mal's fight against the Darkling serves as the backdrop for their romantic and personal growth.

A critical plot point in fantasy romance is the moment of sacrifice or trial, where one or both protagonists must make a significant sacrifice for the sake of love or the greater good. This moment is pivotal because it tests the strength and sincerity of the protagonists' feelings for each other, often against a fantastical setting or scenario. For example, in *The Wrath & the Dawn* by Renée Ahdieh, Shahrzad volunteers to marry the caliph, not out of love, but as a sacrificial attempt to end his reign of terror, only to find her heart conflicted by the unexpected depth of their connection.

The journey or quest is another essential plot point in fantasy romance, serving as both a literal and metaphorical journey toward understanding and love. Throughout this journey, the protagonists encounter challenges that reveal their deepest fears and desires, forging a bond that transcends the ordinary. This quest often involves seeking magical artifacts, unraveling ancient mysteries, or undertaking a perilous journey across enchanted lands, each step bringing the characters closer to each other and the resolution of the central conflict. *In Serpent & Dove* by Shelby Mahurin, the reluctant alliance and subsequent journey of Lou and Reid drive the plot forward and serve as a crucible for their relationship.

Finally, the culmination of the fantasy and romance arcs in a unified climax is a hallmark of the genre. This convergence sees the resolution of the fantastical conflict intertwined with the fulfillment of the romantic relationship, affirming the power of love amidst the backdrop of epic fantasy. Whether it's a battle against dark forces, the breaking of a curse, or the fulfillment of a prophecy, the climax resolves the protagonists' external and internal conflicts, sealing their destinies together in a way that satisfies both the fantasy and romance narratives. In *The Queen of Nothing* by Holly Black, the climactic confrontation not only determines the fate of Faerie but also brings Jude and Cardan's tumultuous relationship to a head, showcasing the unique ability of fantasy romance to weave together grandiose and intimate storytelling.

* * *

Symbolism enriches narrative depth and enhances thematic resonance, acting as a conduit through which deeper layers of meaning are conveyed in literature. Using symbols, authors can imbue their narratives with a complexity that transcends the literal, offering readers a richer, more immersive experience. In storytelling, symbols often manifest as objects, characters, settings, or motifs that carry significance beyond their surface appearance, illuminating themes, emotions, and character arcs in a subtle yet powerful manner.

In fantasy literature, symbolism is particularly potent, as the genre's inherent detachment from reality allows for a broader exploration of abstract concepts through tangible means. For instance, light and darkness can symbolize the eternal struggle between good and evil, knowledge and ignorance, or hope and despair. J.R.R. Tolkien's *The Lord of the Rings* employs this dichotomy to great effect, with the light of Galadriel's phial serving as a beacon of hope and courage in the face of the enveloping darkness of Mordor. This symbolic use of light not only reinforces the thematic underpinnings of the narrative but also offers a visual and emotional anchor for the reader's journey through Middle Earth.

Water is another symbol rich with interpretive possibilities, often representing life, renewal, or the unconscious. In literature, rivers, seas, and rain can symbolize the passage of time, the flow of destiny, or the cleansing of past sins. In Madeline Miller's *Circe*, the sea is a constant presence, reflecting Circe's isolation and tumultuous emotional state, symbolizing her strength and the transformative power of her journey. The sea's dual nature as life-giving and perilous mirrors the complexity of Circe's existence between the worlds of gods and mortals.

Animals and mythical creatures frequently serve symbolic roles, embodying human traits, divine messages, or societal values. The use of animals as symbols can range from representing specific qualities, such as an owl's wisdom or a dog's loyalty, to more complex allegorical functions. In George Orwell's *Animal Farm*, animals embody political ideologies and historical figures, critiquing the corruption of revolutionary ideals through the allegory of a farmyard rebellion. This symbolic use of animals allows Orwell to explore themes of power, manipulation, and freedom in a manner that is both accessible and deeply poignant.

The seasons and the natural cycle are often imbued with symbolic significance, reflecting the passage of time, cycles of growth and decay, and the characters' internal states. Spring can symbolize rebirth and new beginnings, while autumn might represent maturity, loss, or the approach of death. In Laini Taylor's *Daughter of Smoke and Bone*, the changing seasons underscore the evolution of the protagonist's journey and the shifting dynamics of the world around her, mirroring the cycles of conflict and renewal that define the narrative.

Color symbolism offers authors a versatile tool for conveying mood, character, and theme. Specific colors can evoke certain emotions, denote cultural associations, or highlight contrasts between characters and settings. Red, for example, can symbolize passion, danger, or sacrifice, imbuing scenes or objects with a depth of meaning that resonates with the reader on an instinctual level. In *The Red Tent* by Anita Diamant, the titular tent and the color red serve as powerful symbols of femininity, blood, and the shared experiences of women, weaving a rich tapestry of connection and tradition that forms the heart of the narrative.

Through the strategic use of symbolism, authors craft layers of meaning that enrich the narrative, inviting readers to engage with the text on a deeper, more interpretive level. Symbolism bridges the gap between the concrete and the abstract, offering a medium through which the complexities of human experience, emotion, and thought are explored and expressed. In doing so, it not only enhances the thematic richness of the story but also deepens the reader's emotional and intellectual engagement with the work.

Chapter 16

Weaving Themes & Motifs

Weaving themes and motifs into the rich tapestry of fantasy romance requires a delicate balance, a nuanced understanding of genre conventions, and a creative vision that can transcend them. Themes in fantasy romance often explore the intersection of love and power, the conflict between destiny and free will, and the transformative nature of love. Motifs, recurring symbols, or elements that reinforce these themes serve as threads that bind the narrative, enriching the story with layers of meaning that resonate with readers on a deeper level.

One classic theme in fantasy romance is the power of love to transcend boundaries, whether they be societal norms, physical barriers, or even the laws of magic. Motifs such as star-crossed lovers or enchanted items that symbolize the lovers' connection often highlight this theme. For example, in *Romeo and Juliet*, the motif of the divided families underscores the theme of love's power to challenge societal constraints. In a fantasy setting, this might be represented by a magical locket that allows two lovers from warring factions to communicate, symbolizing their love's ability to bridge divides.

Another prevalent theme is the exploration of destiny versus free will, where characters grapple with prophecies or fates that seem to dictate their paths, particularly in matters of the heart. Motifs that frequently accompany this theme include recurring dreams, cycles of the moon, or ancient texts, each echoing the tension between predetermined paths and the characters' desires to forge their own destinies. In *The Night Circus* by Erin Morgenstern, the motif of the clock, with its intricate mechanics and predetermined motion, mirrors the characters' struggles against the seemingly inescapable destiny laid out for them, emphasizing the theme of free will within the confines of fate.

The transformative power of love, a theme at the heart of many fantasy romances, suggests that love can change individuals, alter destinies, and even reshape worlds. Motifs commonly accompanying this theme include the changing seasons to represent growth and renewal or alchemical symbols to signify the transformation process. In *A Court of Thorns and Roses* by Sarah J. Maas, the seasonal courts of the faerie realms serve as a motif that underscores the theme of transformation, reflecting the protagonist's personal growth and the evolving nature of her love.

The conflict between the magical and the mundane offers another rich vein for thematic exploration, where the intrusion of the fantastical into the characters' lives tests the strength of their love and understanding of the world. Motifs such as hidden doors or secret worlds can symbolize the threshold between the known and the unknown, highlighting the theme of the magical encroaching upon the everyday. In *Outlander* by Diana Gabaldon, the standing stones that enable time travel serve as a motif for this theme, representing the portal between different worlds and times and the impact of the fantastical on the protagonists' romance.

Sacrifice is a theme often woven into the fabric of fantasy romance, where love demands the ultimate price, whether it be personal happiness, power, or even life itself. The motif of the sacrificial altar or a ceremonial knife can underscore this theme, symbolizing the acts of giving up something precious for the greater good or the sake of love. In *The Hunger Games* by Suzanne Collins, the recurring motif of the Mockingjay pin becomes a symbol of sacrifice and rebellion, echoing the protagonist's willingness to sacrifice herself for those she loves and the greater cause.

The theme of forbidden love, where societal laws, ancient curses, or fundamental differences challenge the lovers' union, is a staple of fantasy romance. This theme is often accompanied by motifs of barriers, such as walls or chasms, representing the divide between the lovers. In *Romeo and Juliet*, the balcony scene serves as a powerful forbidden love motif, symbolizing the physical and emotional barriers that separate the star-crossed lovers.

Rebirth and renewal, themes that speak to the cyclical nature of life and love, can be highlighted through motifs such as the phoenix, symbolizing resurrection, or spring flowers, representing new beginnings. In *Harry Potter and the Deathly Hallows* by J.K. Rowling, the phoenix motif is closely tied to themes of rebirth and the enduring nature of love, as characters are reborn through sacrifice and love persists beyond death.

The duality of light and darkness is a motif often used to explore themes of knowledge and ignorance, good and evil, or love and hate. This motif can be manifested in the contrasting settings of sunlit meadows and shadowed forests or in characters who embody these dual aspects. In *The Lord of the Rings* by J.R.R. Tolkien, the interplay of light and darkness serves as a backdrop to the characters' journey, symbolizing the struggle between hope and despair and the power of love and fellowship to illuminate the darkest paths.

With its capacity for both destruction and renewal, water serves as a motif to explore themes of emotional depth, purification, and change. Rivers, seas, and rain can symbolize life's ebb and flow, the cleansing of past wounds, or the characters' emotional journeys. In *The Shape of Water* by Guillermo del Toro and Daniel Kraus, water becomes a central motif, symbolizing the transformative power of love and the fluidity of identity and acceptance.

Finally, the motif of the journey, whether it be a quest in search of a magical artifact or a pilgrimage of self-discovery, underscores themes of adventure, personal growth, and the pursuit of love. The road traveled by the protagonists symbolizes their evolving relationship, marked by trials, revelations, and moments of connection. In *The Princess Bride* by William Goldman, the motif of the journey encapsulates the theme of love's endurance and the adventures that shape the characters' bond.

By thoughtfully incorporating motifs that enhance the fantasy and romantic elements, authors can deepen the thematic richness of their narratives, creating fantasy romance stories that resonate with timeless truths and capture the imagination of readers. Through this intricate dance of themes and motifs, the genre transcends mere escapism, offering profound insights into the nature of love, power, and destiny.

Chapter 17

POV and Tense

Choosing the point of view (POV) and tense is a pivotal decision that shapes the entire narrative structure, influencing how readers perceive the story, connect with characters, and experience the unfolding romance and fantasy elements. Each POV and tense brings unique strengths and challenges, impacting the intimacy, immediacy, and scope of the story being told.

First-person POV offers an intimate glimpse into the protagonist's thoughts, feelings, and motivations, creating a direct connection between the character and the reader. This immediacy can be particularly effective in fantasy romance, where the emotional depth of the romantic relationship and the personal stakes in the fantastical elements are central to the narrative. For example, in *The Hunger Games* by Suzanne Collins, the first-person present tense allows readers to experience Katniss's thoughts and feelings in real time, heightening the tension and emotional investment in her survival and relationships.

Third-person limited POV, on the other hand, offers flexibility in focusing on the inner worlds of multiple characters while maintaining a degree of narrative control and focus. This POV can deepen the romantic plot by providing insights into the thoughts and feelings of both love interests, enriching the reader's understanding of their dynamics and conflicts. In *A Court of Thorns and Roses* by Sarah J. Maas, the third-person POV allows for a detailed exploration of the fantastical world and its politics while delving into the central romance's complexities.

Third-person omniscient POV broadens the narrative scope, allowing the author to present a panoramic view of the story's world, including insights into multiple characters, settings, and subplots. This POV can add layers of complexity to the fantasy aspect of the story, weaving together various narrative threads into a cohesive tapestry. However, it can sometimes distance readers from the emotional core of the romance unless skillfully balanced with moments of close narrative focus on the protagonists' internal experiences.

The choice of tense also significantly impacts the storytelling. Present tense can imbue the narrative with a sense of immediacy and urgency, making each moment feel vivid and consequential. This can be particularly engaging in scenes of high action or emotional intensity, with high stakes for fantasy and romance elements. For instance, *The Night Circus* by Erin Morgenstern uses the present tense to enhance the magical, dreamlike quality of the narrative, drawing readers into the immediate experience of its enchanting world and the slow-burning romance.

Past tense, the more traditional choice, offers a sense of reflection and narrative breadth, allowing for a more expansive exploration of the characters' journeys and the development of the romance over time. It can provide a sense of inevitability or destiny to the romantic arc as the story is recounted with hindsight. In *Outlander* by Diana Gabaldon, the use of past tense allows for a richly detailed historical setting and a deep exploration of the characters' evolving relationship, lending the narrative a sense of depth and timelessness.

The impact of POV on storytelling extends beyond the narrative technique, influencing the reader's emotional engagement, the plot's pacing, and the depth of the worldbuilding. A carefully chosen POV can draw readers closer to the characters, making their triumphs and tribulations more impactful and immersing them more fully in the fantastical world of the story. It shapes the lens through which the events are viewed, coloring the narrative with the unique perceptions and biases of the narrator(s), affecting how readers interpret the story.

Deciding on the tense for a fantasy romance involves considering the type of engagement the author wishes to create with the reader. Present tense might be chosen to make the story feel more immediate and immersive, inviting readers to experience events and emotions alongside the characters. This can be particularly effective in conveying the intensity of the romantic connection and the immediacy of the characters' unbelievable challenges.

Conversely, past tense might be preferred for its ability to convey a broader narrative scope and a more reflective tone, offering readers a sense of journeying through the story alongside the narrator. This can lend a timeless quality to the romance, suggesting that the love story is one for the ages while also allowing for complex world-building and backstory to be woven into the narrative.

The choice of POV and tense is a strategic decision that shapes the narrative's voice, tone, and perspective. It determines how closely readers align with the characters, how the story unfolds in time, and how the fantastical and romantic elements are experienced. Through carefully considering these narrative tools, authors can craft fantasy romance stories that captivate and resonate, inviting readers into worlds where love and magic intertwine in profound and memorable ways.

* * *

Utilizing multiple points of view (POVs) in fantasy romance offers a dynamic narrative approach that can enrich the storytelling experience, though it also introduces specific challenges that authors must navigate. The decision to incorporate multiple perspectives significantly impacts the narrative's structure, pacing, and emotional depth. This approach can greatly enhance the complexity and richness of the story, providing a multifaceted view of the fantastical world and its romantic relationships.

One of the major advantages of using multiple POVs in fantasy romance is the ability to offer a broader under-standing of the world and its magical systems. By presenting the story through the eyes of different characters, authors can explore diverse aspects of the setting and culture, delivering a more rounded and immersive experi-ence. This technique allows for a detailed exploration of the fantasy elements that single POV narratives might struggle to convey without extensive exposition. For example, in Game of Thrones by George R.R. Martin, the multiple POV structure enables a vast exploration of the Seven Kingdoms, providing insights into the world's political, social, and magical complexities.

Furthermore, multiple POVs can deepen the emotional and relational dynamics of the story, offering readers a more comprehensive understanding of the characters' motivations, fears, and desires. This is particularly beneficial in romance, where the emotional stakes are high, and understanding the internal landscapes of both parties in a relationship can significantly enhance the reader's investment and satisfaction. By witnessing the thoughts and feelings of both lovers, readers gain a more nuanced appreciation of the romance, as seen in *Six of Crows* by Leigh Bardugo, where the shifting perspectives enrich the narrative with complex emotional layers and diverse romantic subplots.

However, one of the challenges of employing multiple POVs is maintaining a clear and coherent narrative thread. With the story shifting between different perspectives, there's a risk of fragmenting the narrative or diluting the tension and pacing. Authors must skillfully balance the various viewpoints, ensuring that each one advances the story and contributes to developing the plot and characters. This requires careful planning and consideration to avoid confusing readers or detracting from the central romance and fantasy themes.

Another potential drawback is achieving equal depth and development for all POV characters. In a genre where readers often seek deep emotional connections with the protagonists, spreading the narrative focus too thinly can result in underdeveloped characters or relationships lacking depth. This can be particularly challenging in fantasy romance, where the development of the romantic relationship is crucial to the reader's engagement. Ensuring that each POV character's arc is fully realized and contributes meaningfully to the romance and fantasy elements is essential for maintaining narrative cohesion and emotional impact.

Additionally, managing reader attachment and satisfaction with multiple POVs can be complex. While some readers appreciate the depth and breadth that multiple perspectives can bring to a story, others may find themselves more attached to certain characters, feeling frustrated or disengaged when the narrative shifts away from their favorites. Balancing the distribution of narrative time and ensuring that each POV shift feels warranted and engaging is essential to keep readers invested throughout the story.

In conclusion, while multiple POVs in fantasy romance can offer a richly layered and expansive narrative, the approach requires careful execution to maximize its benefits and mitigate its challenges. By thoughtfully integrating multiple perspectives, authors can create a compelling, immersive world that captures the complexity of romance and magic, offering readers a multifaceted experience that resonates on multiple levels.

Chapter 18

Engaging Openings & Setting the Tone Early

Crafting an engaging opening for your fantasy romance novel is akin to casting a spell that ensnares the reader's imagination from the very first line. Your task is to weave a beginning that not only captivates but also introduces the fantastical elements of your world with a delicate balance of intrigue and clarity. This initial invitation into your story's universe is crucial; it sets the tone, establishes the setting, and ignites the spark of romance that will burn throughout your narrative. As you embark on this endeavor, imagine yourself at the threshold of a hidden realm, ready to guide your reader into the wonders and mysteries that lie beyond.

* * *

Begin with an opening scene that drops the reader into the heart of your fantasy world, but do so with a sense of mystery and anticipation. Consider starting in medias res, where action or a pivotal moment unfolds with little preamble. This technique can immediately immerse the reader in the unique aspects of your world, whether it's a bustling market in an ancient city where magic simmers beneath the surface or a forbidden forest where mythical creatures roam. Yet, amidst this action, introduce a hint of the romance that will thread through your narrative—a longing glance across a crowded square or a fateful collision that entwines the destinies of your protagonists.

* * *

Employ vivid, sensory details to bring your fantasy world to life from the outset. Your opening paragraphs should paint a picture so vivid that readers can almost smell the incense in the air, feel the cobblestones beneath their feet, or hear the distant call of an unknown beast. However, the art lies in doing so without overwhelming the reader with exposition. Weave these details naturally into the action or the characters' observations to create a backdrop that feels alive and pulsating with magic. This not only grounds the reader in your world but also stirs a sense of wonder and curiosity about the land you've crafted and the love story about to unfold within it.

* * *

Introduce your protagonist in a way that immediately endears them to the reader or piques interest in their plight. Whether your hero or heroine is caught in a situation that showcases their strength, cunning, or vulnerability, make sure it also hints at their deeper desires or fears. This initial glimpse into their character should foreshadow their journey, both in the fantastical realm and in the realm of the heart. If your story is told from multiple POVs, consider carefully whose perspective will offer the most compelling introduction to the world and the emerging romance.

* * *

Incorporate a hint of the central conflict or the magical elements that will drive your plot. This could be as subtle as a whispered rumor of war, a mysterious curse mentioned in passing, or a mystical phenomenon that disrupts the ordinary flow of life. The key is to intrigue without revealing too much too soon, laying breadcrumbs that lead the reader deeper into the story. This initial brush with the fantastical serves not only to anchor your romance in its unique setting but also to entice the reader with the promise of adventure and enchantment.

The opening of your fantasy romance should subtly weave in the themes that will resonate throughout your story— themes of love conquering adversity, the search for identity in a vast and varied world, or the balance between power and compassion. These thematic undercurrents, introduced early on, will enrich the narrative and give depth to the burgeoning romance. Whether through an ominous prophecy, a legend recounted by elders, or a personal vow made by the protagonist, these themes will serve as the soul of your story, guiding the reader's journey through your fantastical world and the hearts of your characters.

Crafting an opening that captivates and introduces your fantasy world is your first enchantment as a storyteller, requiring both artistry and precision. As you pen these initial lines, remember that you are not just creating a story but inviting readers into a world where magic is real and love is the greatest adventure. Let your opening be the key that unlocks the gate to this realm, promising the reader that beyond lies a tale of wonder, peril, and passion that will linger with them long after the final page is turned.

* * *

Setting the tone for romance early in a narrative is akin to laying the foundation for a house; it's essential for building anticipation and guiding the reader's expectations. From the first few pages, your narrative should whisper promises of the love story that's about to unfold. This can be achieved through subtle exchanges, descriptive passages that hint at longing, or the immediate chemistry between characters. Imagine a scene lit in the twilight, where two potential lovers meet under anything but ordinary circumstances. Their initial interaction, perhaps with a mix of curiosity and wariness, sets the stage for a romance that promises to be both complex and captivating.

To infuse your opening with romance, consider employing language that evokes the senses and stirs emotions. Descriptions of the environment, characters' appearances, and the electric tension of first encounters can all be imbued with a romantic lens. For instance, the way the moonlight dances in a character's hair or the intoxicating scent of a night-blooming garden can serve as metaphors for the burgeoning attraction between your protagonists. These details not only enrich the setting but also subtly signal to readers that love will be a central theme of the story.

* * *

Introducing conflict and intrigue from the outset is crucial for maintaining narrative momentum and ensuring the romance does not exist in a vacuum. Conflict serves as the catalyst for character development and plot advancement, presenting obstacles that the protagonists must overcome, individually and together. This could manifest as a rivalry between factions, a forbidden love, or personal vendettas threatening to tear the lovers apart. By weaving in elements of conflict early on, you create stakes that add depth to the romance, transforming it from a simple attraction to a love worth fighting for.

Intrigue plays a complementary role to conflict, providing the mystery and suspense that keep readers turning the pages. Introduce secrets, hidden pasts, or unsolved mysteries intricately linked to the romantic plot. Perhaps one of the lovers is harboring a secret that could change everything, or there's a prophecy looming over their heads, shrouded in mystery. The key is to intertwine this intrigue with the romantic arc so that solving the mystery or unveiling the secret becomes integral to the development of the relationship.

* * *

Balancing the tone of romance with the introduction of conflict and intrigue requires a delicate touch. The plot's complexities should not overshadow the romance, nor should the intrigue detract from the emotional authenticity of the love story. Achieving this balance means crafting scenes where the development of the romance and the unfolding of the plot are mutually reinforcing. For instance, a shared quest can serve as a backdrop for deepening the protagonists' bond, with each challenge bringing them closer together, even as it tests their resolve.

Character interactions are vital for setting the tone of romance and intrigue. Dialogue, in particular, can build tension, reveal character dynamics, and propel the plot forward. Banter can hint at underlying attractions, while heated exchanges might reveal deeper conflicts or secrets. Through their interactions, characters can express their desires, fears, and motivations, laying bare the emotional stakes of the romance and the overarching narrative.

The narrative voice also plays a significant role in setting the tone. A first-person POV can offer intimate insights into a character's feelings and thoughts about the other, weaving in internal monologues that ponder the nature of their attraction or the barriers to their love. Alternatively, a third-person omniscient POV can provide a broader perspective, offering glimpses into the hearts and minds of all involved, painting a fuller picture of the romantic and intrigue-filled landscape.

Setting the tone for romance and intrigue involves planting seeds that will grow throughout the narrative. Early hints at attraction, moments of vulnerability, and the introduction of mysteries should foreshadow future developments. This not only creates anticipation but also ensures that the romance feels earned and the resolution of the intrigue satisfying. The initial chapters should promise readers that their investment in the characters' journey will be rewarded with a story that weaves together love, conflict, and mystery in a tapestry as rich and complex as life itself.

Chapter 19

Building Romantic Tension

Building romantic tension in a fantasy setting requires a nuanced blend of narrative elements, where the burgeoning romance between characters unfolds against a backdrop rich with magic, mystery, and danger. The initial spark of attraction, perhaps kindled under the light of a blood moon or amidst the ruins of an ancient spell-bound castle, sets the stage for a dance of desire and denial that captivates readers. This tension is the heartbeat of the romance, pulsating through every glance, touch, and whispered secret, intensified by the extraordinary circumstances only a fantasy world can provide.

One effective technique for escalating romantic tension is the use of proximity forced by the fantasy setting itself. Imagine our protagonists bound by a spell that requires them to remain within a certain distance of each other or a quest that throws them into the depths of a labyrinthine forest filled with enchantments. This enforced closeness can amplify the characters' awareness of each other, turning every interaction into a charged moment that teases the possibility of more. The constant push and pull, driven by their shared circumstances, stokes the flames of attraction even as they navigate the perils of their journey.

Fantasy elements complicate the romance, introducing barriers that test the strength and depth of the characters' feelings. A curse that forbids touch, a prophecy foretelling doom should they unite, or loyalties to warring magical factions can all drive a wedge between the lovers. These fantastical obstacles underscore the forbidden or doomed nature of their love, making every stolen moment all the more precious and fraught with consequence. The struggle to overcome these magical barriers heightens the tension, as the characters must choose between their hearts and the greater good.

Conversely, fantasy elements can also facilitate the romance, creating scenarios that bring the characters closer together. A shared power that grows stronger with their emotional bond, a dream realm where they meet in secret, away from prying eyes, or a mythical creature that recognizes them as soulmates can all underscore their union's inevitability. These magical affirmations of their connection can provide moments of respite and intimacy amidst the conflict, reinforcing the romantic tension even as they offer hope for a resolution.

Maintaining tension through obstacles and conflicts is crucial for keeping readers engaged. Introducing a rival love interest, perhaps a prince from a neighboring kingdom or a warrior from one's own ranks can inject a sense of urgency and jealousy into the narrative. This triangle, especially when entangled with political intrigue or a quest of great importance, can force the protagonists to confront their feelings for each other, even as they navigate the complexities of their positions.

The revelation of secrets or hidden pasts is another technique that can effectively maintain and escalate romantic tension. Discovering that one lover has been keeping a secret—maybe an identity hidden beneath spells or a pact with a dark entity—can introduce a sense of betrayal and hurt that the characters must work through. Uncovering the truth, forgiving, and understanding add layers to their relationship, deepening the emotional resonance of the romance.

External conflicts, such as battles against dark forces, political machinations that seek to exploit their love for strategic gain, or the threat of an ancient evil awakening, also maintain tension. These conflicts test the characters' commitment to each other, forcing them to make difficult choices that could either doom or cement their relationship. The looming sense of danger, combined with the uncertainty of survival, makes every moment they choose to spend together an act of defiance against the chaos encroaching upon their world.

Incorporating moments of vulnerability and sacrifice amid these tensions and obstacles can significantly heighten the romantic stakes. A scene where one character risks everything to save the other, revealing the depth of their love, can be a turning point, transforming the simmering tension into a declaration of commitment. These acts of love, set against the backdrop of a fantastical world where the cost is often life or death, underscore the intensity of their feelings, making the romance all the more compelling.

Utilizing the fantasy setting itself as a character in the romance can add an additional layer of tension. The world's inherent dangers, beauty, and mysteries can mirror the tumultuous journey of the protagonists' relationship. For instance, a city divided by magical barriers can symbolize the divide between lovers, with each venture across the boundaries serving as a metaphor for overcoming the obstacles to their love.

The pacing of the narrative plays a crucial role in maintaining romantic tension. Balancing moments of high action or dramatic revelation with quieter, intimate scenes allows the relationship to develop at a believable pace. Slow-burning romance, where characters gradually peel away layers of mistrust or prejudice, can be particularly effective in a fantasy setting, where the world-building and plot complexity allow the romance to mature.

Finally, the resolution of romantic tension should feel earned, culminating in the characters' journey through a landscape marked by magic, conflict, and sacrifice. Whether it ends in heartbreak or happily ever after, the conclusion should reflect the characters' growth and the world they inhabit. Crafting a satisfying resolution requires a delicate balance, tying up the narrative threads of both the fantasy and romantic elements in a way that honors the journey the characters and readers have undertaken together.

In weaving together themes of fantasy and romance, authors create a narrative alchemy that captivates and enchants. The interplay between the fantastical setting and the emotional depth of the romance offers readers an escape into worlds where love is both a challenge and a magic of its own, making the journey all the more rewarding.

Chapter 20

Seamless World-Building in Narrative Pace

Seamless world-building in fantasy romance is akin to crafting a delicate tapestry, where each thread of narrative and descriptive detail must be woven together with care, creating a vivid, immersive world without sacrificing the momentum of the story. Achieving this balance is a nuanced art, requiring a deep understanding of the genre and the needs of the narrative. The goal is to transport readers into the fantastical world you've created, making them feel as though they're walking its paths and breathing its air, all while keeping them engaged in the unfolding romance and plot.

The first step in seamless world-building is to integrate the fantastical elements naturally into the narrative. Instead of pausing the story for lengthy expositions, sprinkle details of the world and its magic through the characters' interactions, dialogues, and experiences. For instance, as two characters debate their next move in their quest, they might pass by a market where vendors sell enchanted artifacts, providing a glimpse into the everyday magic of the world. This method keeps the pace brisk while still enriching the setting.

Character-driven exploration is a powerful tool for revealing the world without slowing down the story. Through the eyes of the protagonists, especially if one is unfamiliar with the setting, readers can discover the world organically. As the characters navigate challenges, fall in love, or confront their enemies, the setting unfolds around them, revealing its wonders and dangers in a way that feels integral to the narrative. This approach ensures that world-building serves the story, enhancing the romance and conflict rather than detracting from it.

Employing descriptive language judiciously is key to maintaining a narrative pace while building your world. Vivid, concise descriptions that evoke the senses can paint a rich picture of the setting in a few well-chosen words, avoiding the pitfall of bogging down the story with unnecessary detail. For example, a description of a magical forest might focus on the whisper of leaves speaking ancient languages or the soft glow of bioluminescent flowers, providing a sense of wonder without halting the plot's momentum.

The integration of world-building with character development and plot progression also helps to balance descriptive detail with narrative pace. The world's history, culture, and magic can be tied to the characters' backstories, goals, and challenges, making the setting a dynamic element of the story that directly impacts the protagonists' journey. This deepens the reader's immersion in the world and ensures that every detail of the setting moves the story forward.

Incorporating motifs and symbols related to the setting throughout the narrative can subtly reinforce the world-building while keeping the focus on the action and character development. A recurring motif, such as a mythical creature or a significant landscape feature, can serve as a shorthand for larger concepts within the world, enriching the narrative without the need for extensive exposition. This technique allows for a layer of depth that resonates with the reader emotionally, linking the setting intimately to the story's themes and the characters' arcs.

Contrast and conflict within the setting can serve as a method of world-building that naturally complements the narrative pace. By showcasing the differences between regions, cultures, or magical systems within the world, authors can reveal the complexity of their setting through the protagonists' journey. This provides variety and intrigue and frames the world as a character in its own right, with its conflicts and challenges mirroring or complicating the central romance.

Flashbacks and legends, used sparingly, can offer glimpses into the world's history and mythology without interrupting the present narrative flow. These elements, woven into the story's fabric at critical moments, can provide context and depth to the setting and its significance to the characters and plot. For example, a legend recounted by an elder might illuminate the ancient origins of a conflict, enriching the reader's understanding of the stakes without necessitating a detour from the main narrative.

The pacing of world-building reveals is crucial for maintaining engagement. Introducing the most fantastical elements of the setting gradually, in tandem with the development of the romance and plot, ensures that readers are not overwhelmed and that their curiosity is continually piqued. This staggered approach allows for a natural exploration of the world that feels like a discovery alongside the characters, keeping the narrative momentum steady.

Dialogue and internal monologues offer another avenue for integrating world-building seamlessly. Characters can reflect on their surroundings, question the peculiarities of their world, or discuss legends and politics in ways that feel natural and in service to character development or plot advancement. This technique ensures that the world-building is always relevant to the story at hand, enhancing the narrative rather than pausing it.

The emotional resonance of the setting with the protagonists' journey is a subtle yet powerful form of world-building that enriches the narrative without slowing it. When the setting reflects or contrasts the emotional states or themes of the romance—such as a cursed land mirroring a forbidden love—it deepens the reader's emotional investment in both the characters and the world. This form of world-building is evocative and efficient, embedding the setting deeply within the story's heart.

Finally, maintaining a delicate balance between showing and telling in world-building allows for a narrative that feels richly detailed yet briskly paced. Show the world through action, sensory details, and character interactions, and tell only when it clarifies or enhances understanding without detracting from the story's immediacy. This balance ensures that the fantastical setting and the romance at the narrative's core are neither overshadowed nor underdeveloped, captivating the reader with an expansive and deeply personal story.

Chapter 21

Consistency

Consistency in world-building and romantic development is the cornerstone of crafting a compelling fantasy romance narrative. It ensures that the story's fantastical elements harmonize with the evolving romantic relationship, creating a seamless and immersive reading experience. Maintaining consistency involves meticulous planning and attention to detail, ensuring that the rules of the fantasy world are clearly defined and adhered to throughout the narrative. Similarly, the romantic development must progress believably and coherently, with each step in the relationship reflecting the characters' growth and the challenges they face. This consistency strengthens the reader's investment in both the world and the romance, making the story's emotional highs and lows all the more impactful.

Tightening the narrative's pacing is crucial for keeping readers engaged and ensuring that the romantic and fantasy elements have the space to shine. A well-paced story moves smoothly from one plot point to the next, balancing action-packed sequences with quieter moments of character development and romantic tension. By carefully controlling the pacing, authors can prevent the narrative from becoming bogged down in unnecessary details or meandering subplots. This allows for a focused exploration of the fantasy world and the central romance, ensuring that each scene contributes meaningfully to the overall story.

Enhancing the romantic and fantasy elements of the story often involves honing in on the unique aspects of the fantasy setting that can amplify the romance. This might include magical rituals that bring the lovers closer together. These enchanted locations serve as the backdrop for key romantic moments or mythical creatures that play a role in the couple's journey. By weaving these elements more deeply into the narrative, authors can elevate the romance, making it feel integral to the fantasy world rather than an added subplot. This integration enriches the story, making the romance feel as magical and captivating as the world it unfolds in.

Revising character arcs is a critical step in ensuring a satisfying romantic payoff. Characters in fantasy romance must navigate the challenges of the fantastical world and their personal growth and transformation. As the story progresses, their experiences should shape them, preparing them for the culmination of their romantic journey. Revisions might involve deepening the characters' backstories, introducing pivotal moments that test their resolve, or refining their motivations. This ensures that by the time the narrative reaches its climax, the characters have evolved to make the resolution of their romance feel earned and authentic.

Incorporating feedback from early readers or editors is invaluable in identifying areas where the world-building, pacing, or character development may lack consistency or depth. This external perspective can highlight discrepancies in the fantasy world's rules or regions where the romantic development feels rushed or unconvincing. By addressing these issues, authors can strengthen the foundation of their narrative, ensuring that both the fantasy and romance elements are fully realized and seamlessly integrated.

Balancing the exposition necessary for world-building with the forward momentum of the romantic plot requires skillful narrative structuring. Authors might use dialogue, action sequences, or the protagonists' internal reflections to reveal details of the world and its magic without halting the story's progress. This approach keeps the reader engaged, weaving the exposition naturally into the fabric of the narrative and ensuring that the romance remains at the forefront.

Creating moments of vulnerability and connection between the protagonists is essential for deepening the romantic tension and developing their relationship. These moments, whether in the midst of a magical battle or in the quiet after the storm, should reveal new facets of the characters' personalities and feelings for each other. By carefully crafting these interactions, authors can gradually build the emotional stakes of the romance, making the eventual payoff all the more satisfying.

The antagonists and conflicts in the story should directly challenge the protagonists' relationship, testing their commitment and love for each other. Whether it's a rival suitor endowed with magical powers or a societal rule forbidding their union, these obstacles heighten the romantic tension. As the characters struggle to overcome these challenges, their love becomes a beacon of hope and defiance, enriching the narrative with a sense of urgency and depth.

Utilizing the fantasy setting to mirror or symbolize aspects of the protagonists' romantic journey can add layers of meaning to the story. A cursed forest that reflects the characters' fears and doubts or a divided kingdom that symbolizes their seemingly insurmountable differences can serve as powerful metaphors for their relationship. This technique not only enhances the world-building but also ties the romantic development more closely to the fabric of the narrative.

Ensuring that secondary characters and subplots support the main romantic arc is crucial for maintaining narrative focus. These elements should enrich the protagonists' journey, providing contrasts or parallels that underscore the themes of love and sacrifice. By revising the narrative to ensure that every subplot and character contributes to the central romance, authors can create a cohesive and compelling story that captivates readers.

Finally, crafting a climax that brings both the fantasy and romantic elements to a head is key to delivering a satisfying conclusion. This might involve a final showdown where the protagonists must rely on their love to triumph or a sacrifice that cements their bond forever. The culmination of their journey should feel like a natural extension of their growth and the challenges they've faced, offering a resolution that is both emotionally gratifying and true to the world they inhabit. By carefully weaving together the strands of romance and fantasy throughout the narrative, authors can create a story where the payoff feels inevitable and deeply rewarding.

Chapter 22

Solicit Feedback

Seeking feedback is akin to consulting the oracles—navigating the mists of creation to find clarity and direction for your narrative odyssey. This process, integral to honing your craft, involves presenting your woven tapestry of fantastical worlds and heart-stirring romances to a trusted circle of readers or critique partners. Like lanterns in the dark, their insights illuminate areas of strength and shadows of improvement, guiding you toward a more polished and compelling tale. It's a delicate dance of openness, requiring you to lay bare the fruits of your imagination and heed the wisdom offered by those who traverse your created worlds.

Interpreting feedback, especially within the nuanced fantasy romance genre, demands a discerning eye and a receptive heart. Whether it praises the intricacy of your world-building or questions the depth of your lovers' connection, each piece of advice is a gem to be appraised in the light of your artistic vision. To improve the fantastical elements, you might find yourself delving deeper into the lore that underpins your world, ensuring that the magic that flows through your narrative veins does so with consistency and originality. Similarly, feedback on the romantic elements encourages you to explore the emotional landscapes of your characters with greater nuance, weaving their desires, conflicts, and resolutions into a more poignant and resonant love story.

Revising your manuscript based on feedback is a journey of transformation, where the essence of your story is refined and its execution sharpened. This stage is where the alchemy of creation happens—turning leaden passages into golden prose, reshaping the narrative until it sings with the harmony of well-matched lovers and a world that breathes magic. It involves reimagining scenes that fell flat, deepening character arcs that seemed shallow, and perhaps, most importantly, reinforcing the pillars of your story that stand strong. Yet, this process is not about conceding to every suggestion but rather discerning which pieces of feedback align with your story's soul.

Maintaining your vision amidst this sea of voices is the challenge and triumph of a true storyteller. It requires an unwavering belief in the core of your story—the unique melody of your narrative voice that sings of ancient magics and timeless loves. Your vision is the compass that guides your revisions, ensuring that while the feedback informs and improves your tale, it does not steer you away from the truth of your story. It's about finding balance, merging the insightful reflections of your readers with the inner knowing of your creative spirit.

Feedback specific to fantasy romance often touches upon the delicate balance between world-building and character development. Readers and critique partners might point out where the scales tip too heavily toward elaborate descriptions of magical systems at the expense of the central romance or vice versa. This feedback is invaluable, prompting you to weave the fantastical and romantic elements together more seamlessly, ensuring that each kiss is as spellbinding as the world in which it takes place and that every magical conflict is as charged with emotion as with power.

Interpreting feedback might also reveal the need for greater depth in your characters' emotional journeys. In fantasy romance, the stakes are often as high in the heart as they are in the world at large. Feedback highlighting areas where the characters' motivations, fears, or desires feel underexplored is a call to delve deeper and flesh out the internal conflicts and passions that drive them. This deep dive enriches the narrative, making the moments of triumph, sacrifice, and love all the more impactful.

Revising based on feedback while maintaining your vision can feel like navigating a ship through a storm—holding steady to your course while adjusting the sails to harness the wind. It's a test of resilience and adaptability, requiring you to reassess and rework elements of your story without losing sight of its destination. This might mean rewriting entire chapters to capture the essence of the romance better or subtly tweaking the lore of your world to make it more accessible and integrated into the narrative. Each revision is a step closer to realizing the full potential of your story, guided by the feedback but driven by your vision.

The role of feedback in crafting fantasy romance is not just about fixing weaknesses but also about recognizing and amplifying strengths. Positive feedback, highlighting moments where the romance tugs at the heartstrings or the fantasy enchants the imagination, serves as an affirmation of your story's power. It encourages you to lean into these strengths, to replicate and expand upon what resonates with readers, ensuring that your story improves and shines with its unique light.

Seeking feedback is an act of bravery, interpreting it as an act of wisdom and revising based on it as an act of dedication. This iterative process is fundamental to the craft of storytelling, especially in the intricate dance of fantasy romance, where every detail contributes to the spell you cast upon your readers. It's a journey that demands much from you as a creator—patience, humility, and courage—but the reward is a story that lives and breathes with the magic of new worlds and the depth of true love.

Maintaining your vision throughout this process ensures that your fantasy romance remains authentically yours. It's the guarantee that despite the weaving of external insights and suggestions, the story that emerges is one only you can tell. Your vision is the soul of your narrative, the spark that ignites the magic and romance within your pages. Balancing feedback with this vision is the key to crafting a story that not only captivates and enchants but also endures in the hearts of your readers.

Chapter 23

Editing

Editing for clarity in the intertwined realms of fantasy elements and romantic arcs is a meticulous task that demands a keen eye for detail and a deep understanding of narrative harmony. The magic of a fantasy romance novel lies in its ability to transport readers to otherworldly realms and in the emotional resonance of its central love story. Achieving clarity involves refining the fantastical components to enhance rather than overshadow the romance, ensuring that the rules of magic and the contours of the world are conveyed with precision and simplicity. Simultaneously, the romantic arc must be honed to resonate with authenticity, and its milestones and conflicts must be presented with enough depth to engage the reader fully.

Balancing the technical aspects of storytelling with creative expression is akin to walking a tightrope. On one side lies the need for a solid structure, a coherent plot, and well-defined world-building; on the other, the imperative to captivate with lyrical prose, vivid imagery, and moments of profound emotional impact. This balance is crucial in fantasy romance, where the technicalities of magic systems and world lore must seamlessly integrate with the unfolding romance. The editing process should thus focus on ensuring that the exposition of fantasy elements serves the narrative without becoming cumbersome and that the romantic developments flow naturally from the characters' interactions and growth.

Genre-specific considerations play a significant role in the editing process for fantasy romance. The genre demands a unique blend of world-building and character-driven storytelling, where the fantastical and the romantic are equally compelling. Editors and authors must pay close attention to the conventions and expectations of the genre—such as the presence of a believable magical system, the exploration of themes like destiny versus choice, and the development of a romance that feels epic and intimate. Balancing these elements requires a nuanced approach to editing, where both the grandeur of the fantasy setting and the depth of the romantic connection are given room to shine.

One of the key challenges in editing fantasy romance is ensuring that the fantasy elements enhance the romantic arc without overwhelming it. The magic and mythology of the world should provide a backdrop that amplifies the stakes of the romance, offering obstacles and aids that test and strengthen the lovers' bond. This might involve revising scenes to align better the development of the magical plot with key moments in the romantic relationship, ensuring that each fantastical encounter or revelation also serves as a step in the characters' journey toward each other.

Similarly, editing for clarity in the romantic arc involves untangling any convoluted plot threads that might distract from or dilute the central relationship. The emotional progression of the romance should be clear and compelling, with each character's motivations, fears, and desires articulated in a way that resonates with the reader. This might mean refining dialogue to reveal deeper layers of character or adjusting pacing to allow significant moments of connection or conflict to unfold with maximum impact.

In balancing technical aspects with creative storytelling, editors and authors must consider the narrative's pacing. Fantasy romance often involves complex plots with multiple subplots, and maintaining a rhythm that keeps readers engaged without rushing through the world-building or the development of the romance is key. This might involve cutting extraneous scenes that do not serve the dual purpose of advancing the plot, deepening the romantic tension, or adding moments that allow for character reflection and emotional growth.

Attention to language and style is another critical aspect of editing in fantasy romance. The prose should evoke the wonder of the fantasy world and the intensity of the romantic connection without slipping into purple prose. This requires a delicate touch in editing, refining the language to strike the perfect balance between descriptive richness and narrative clarity. The goal is to immerse readers in the story, using language that enhances the mood and tone without distracting from the plot or character development.

Dialogue editing in fantasy romance deserves special attention, as it is a crucial tool for character development and plot advancement. Dialogue between the romantic leads can build tension, reveal secrets, and deepen the connection between characters. Editing should ensure that each exchange rings true to the characters' voices and the setting, contributing to the overall tapestry of the story without feeling forced or out of place.

Character arc revisions are particularly important in fantasy romance, where the protagonists' growth is often linked to the story's fantastical and romantic elements. Editing should focus on ensuring that the characters evolve believable, with their transformations closely tied to the narrative events and the development of their relationship. This might involve strengthening the motivations behind the characters' actions or providing clearer emotional arcs that resonate with the story's themes.

Integrating subplots and secondary characters in the editing process also requires careful consideration. In fantasy romance, subplots can enrich the world and add layers to the narrative, but they should not detract from the central romance. Editing should aim to weave these elements into the main storyline to complement and enhance the romantic arc, ensuring that each subplot contributes to the overall narrative cohesion.

Finally, editing for clarity in fantasy romance involves a constant dialogue between preserving the author's creative vision and ensuring the story remains accessible and engaging to readers. This delicate balance is achieved through a deep understanding of genre conventions, a respect for the intricacies of the fantasy world and the emotional depth of the romance, and a commitment to crafting a narrative that enchants and enthralls from the first page to the last. Through meticulous editing, the magical and the romantic are interlaced into a story that captivates the heart and the imagination, offering readers an unforgettable journey into realms of wonder and passion.

Chapter 24

Cover Design, Blurbs and Branding

Cover design is the first invitation to the reader, a visual whisper of the adventures within the pages of a fantasy romance novel. For a genre that weaves the ethereal beauty of fantasy with the deep resonance of romance, the cover must strike a perfect harmony between these elements. It often features imagery that evokes the magical setting of the story—enchanted forests, ancient castles, or mystical arti- facts—blended with visual cues of the central romance, such as entwined figures or a meaningful glance between characters. This fusion promises potential readers a journey not just through a realm of imagination but also through the complexities of the heart.

Color palette choice plays a crucial role in conveying the mood and tone of the fantasy romance genre. Soft pastels might suggest a tale of tender love and magic, while bold, saturated colors could hint at a story of passionate romance and dark spells. The colors must reflect the essence of the narrative, setting the stage for the emotional and fantastical journey that awaits. A well-chosen palette can evoke feelings of wonder, anticipation, and the ineffable connection between lovers destined to find each other in a world of magic and mystery.

Typography on the cover is another critical element, marrying aesthetics with genre expectations. The font choice should complement the imagery, adding to the overall allure without overwhelming it. Elegant, flowing scripts can suggest the timeless beauty of love and the intricate dance of magic, while more straightforward, bold fonts might speak to a tale of fierce devotion and epic battles. The typography serves to make the title and author's name stand out and subtly reinforce the thematic elements of fantasy and romance that define the story.

Writing a blurb that captures the essence of fantasy and romance is an art form. It must entice with hints of the world's wonders and the allure of the romantic plot without revealing too much. The opening lines should draw readers in with a glimpse of the setting or the central conflict, setting the stage for a narrative that spans the spectrums of both genres. Following this, the blurb should introduce the protagonists, hinting at their roles in the fantastical world and the nature of their relationship—whether it's a forbidden love, a bond forged in adversity, or a partnership that could change the fate of their world.

The blurb must also hint at the stakes—what the characters stand to lose, both in the fantasy plot and their personal emotional journey. This dual focus ensures that potential readers understand that the heart of the story lies in the intersection of epic fantasy and deep, meaningful romance. Crafting a blurb that balances these elements without becoming overly complex requires a deep understanding of what draws readers to the genre: the promise of escape to a world of beauty and danger and the enduring power of love.

The synergy between the cover design and the blurb is paramount in conveying the genre correctly through visual and textual elements. They must work together to create a cohesive message that resonates with fantasy romance fans. This means aligning the tone and themes the imagery suggests with the narrative hints provided in the blurb. For instance, if the cover features a dark, foreboding castle shrouded in mist, the blurb should reflect the story's darker tones and the challenges the lovers will face, weaving together their fight against external forces with their battle for their love.

Marketing materials, from bookmarks to posters, extend the visual and textual themes established by the cover and blurb. These materials should echo the magical and romantic elements, using similar color schemes, fonts, and imagery to reinforce the book's identity. This consistency ensures that potential readers are reminded of the unique blend of fantasy and romance that defines the story at every touchpoint, building anticipation and recognition.

Social media campaigns offer a dynamic platform for exploring the themes of fantasy romance through a combination of visuals, teasers, and interactive content. Sharing snippets of the cover art, quotes from the blurb, or character art can create a buzz, allowing readers to immerse themselves in the world of the book even before its release. These campaigns can also highlight the genre's dual appeal, showcasing the fantasy setting's allure and the romance's emotional depth through curated posts that reflect the book's tone and themes.

Author websites and newsletters are another avenue for delving deeper into the elements that make the book a captivating fantasy romance. Exclusive content, such as behind-the-scenes looks at the creation of the cover, discussions about the inspirations for the story's magical world, or insights into the development of the romantic plot, can engage readers on a more personal level. This content reinforces the genre's appeal, providing a richer context for the visual and textual cues in the book's marketing materials.

Though less traditional, book trailers offer a multimedia approach to conveying the essence of fantasy romance. By combining imagery, music, and text, trailers can evoke the atmospheric beauty of the fantasy world and the emotional stakes of the romance. This format allows for a dynamic genre expression, appealing to potential readers' imaginations and hearts in a way that static images and text alone cannot.

At book signings and author events, the thematic elements of fantasy romance can be brought to life through decorations, costumes, or themed activities that reflect the book's setting and romantic plot. These events provide a tangible experience of the story's world, deepening potential readers' interest and engagement.

Finally, engaging directly with the fantasy romance community through forums, book clubs, and conventions can provide invaluable insights into what readers look for in the genre. This interaction can inform future revisions of marketing materials and even influence aspects of the narrative itself, ensuring that the book resonates with its intended audience.

In sum, crafting a narrative and marketing strategy that appeals to fantasy romance readers requires a careful balance of visual and textual elements designed to showcase the unique blend of magic and love that defines the genre. From the cover design to the blurb and through every marketing material in between, the goal is to capture the essence of the story's fantastical and romantic elements, inviting readers into a world where love is as powerful and transformative as the magic that permeates it.

Chapter 25

Resources

Embarking on the journey of writing and appreciating fantasy romance is akin to stepping through a magical portal that leads to endless realms of inspiration, camaraderie, and discovery. As you navigate this enchanting landscape, a trove of resources awaits to guide your path, illuminate your craft, and connect you with fellow adventurers. Here, we chart a course through must-read novels, venerable authors, online havens, and communities that pulse at the heart of fantasy romance, all while whispering words of encouragement for your continual growth in this ever-evolving genre.

The Pillars of Fantasy Romance

The seminal works that have defined and continue to shape the genre are at the foundation of any fantasy romance writer's journey. Novels such as *A Court of Thorns and Roses* by Sarah J. Maas and *The Night Circus* by Erin Morgenstern offer masterclasses in weaving intricate worlds with compelling romantic narratives. These stories, with their richly developed characters and meticulously crafted settings, serve as beacons, guiding aspiring writers in their quest to blend the fantastical with the deeply personal.

Legends and Lorekeepers

The annals of fantasy romance are graced by authors whose pens seem touched by the magic they write about. Juliet Marillier, with her lyrical prose and deep folkloric roots, and Grace Draven, known for her ability to craft believable romance amidst the backdrop of innovative magical systems, stand as titans whose works are essential reading. Their stories are not just tales but tapestries woven with threads of magic, emotion, and the enduring power of love.

Online Grimoires and Guilds

In the digital age, the wisdom and camaraderie sought by fantasy romance writers can often be found in the vast expanse of the internet. Websites like Fantasy-Faction and Romantic Fantasy Shelf offer articles, forums, and reviews that delve into genre-specific writing advice, trends, and book recommendations. These online resources act as modern grimoires, brimming with knowledge and insights accessible with but a few clicks.

The Enchanted Forums

For those seeking a fellowship of like-minded scribes, online forums and social media groups such as Absolute Write's Water Cooler and the Fantasy Romance Alliance provide spaces to share drafts, seek feedback, and discuss the nuances of crafting compelling fantasy romance. Here, in these digital roundtables, writers find not just critique partners but allies and friends, all united by a shared love for the genre.

The Gathering of Scribes

Conventions and writing workshops offer invaluable opportunities for fantasy romance writers to hone their craft, network with industry professionals, and immerse themselves in the vibrant community. Events like the World Fantasy Convention and workshops hosted by the Romance Writers of America (RWA) serve as gatherings where the magic of fantasy romance comes to life, inspiring writers to explore new horizons in their storytelling.

. . .

The Archives of Inspiration

For those seeking guidance from the masters, craft books such as *Steering the Craft* by Ursula K. Le Guin and *Writing Love: Screenwriting Tricks for Authors II* by Alexandra Sokoloff offer insights into storytelling mechanics, character development, and genre-blending. These texts are archives of inspiration, offering tools and techniques to refine one's craft.

The Quest for Originality

In a genre as rich and varied as fantasy romance, the quest for originality is both a challenge and an invitation to innovation. Reading widely across genres, exploring non-Western mythologies, and drawing inspiration from the natural world can fuel the imagination, leading to stories that captivate with their uniqueness and universal appeal.

Embracing the Digital Scroll

The advent of digital publishing and platforms like Wattpad and Archive of Our Own has revolutionized the way fantasy romance stories are shared and discovered. These platforms allow writers to publish their work, receive real-time feedback from readers, and experiment with serialization and novel formats, all within supportive online communities.

.   .   .

The Alchemy of Collaboration

Collaboration with artists, illustrators, and other writers can enrich the fantasy romance writing experience, bringing new dimensions to one's work. Whether through commissioning artwork that brings the story's world to life or co-writing projects that blend diverse voices, these collaborations can be a source of creativity and growth.

Navigating the Labyrinth of Publication

The journey to publication is a labyrinthine adventure, fraught with challenges but also ripe with opportunity. Understanding the landscape of traditional publishing, exploring the realms of self-publishing, and staying informed about the latest trends and market demands are crucial steps. Resources like Writer's Market and industry blogs offer guidance through this maze, helping writers find their path to sharing their stories with the world.

The Enchantment of Marketing

In the digital age, marketing one's fantasy romance novel requires a blend of creativity and strategic thinking. Building an online presence through a well-crafted author website, engaging with readers on social media, and utilizing email newsletters to share updates and exclusive content are essential tactics. The magic of marketing lies in storytelling, not just within the book's pages but in the narrative crafted about the book itself.

The Fellowship of Critique

Feedback from beta readers, critique partners, and editors is invaluable in refining a fantasy romance manuscript. This fellowship offers perspectives that can highlight strengths and identify areas for improvement. Embracing critique with an open heart and a mind focused on growth is essential for honing one's storytelling abilities.

The Continuous Quest for Knowledge

Continuous learning is key to staying relevant and inspired in the ever-evolving landscape of fantasy romance. Attending genre-specific writing workshops, participating in online webinars, and keeping abreast of industry news can fuel a writer's passion and expertise. The quest for knowledge is endless, as each discovery opens the door to new possibilities in storytelling.

. . .

The Resilience of the Heart

Writing fantasy romance is an act of resilience, requiring perseverance through rejection, writer's block, and the myriad challenges accompanying the creative process. It's a testament to the writer's heart, brimming with stories of love and adventure that demand to be told. Embracing resilience, celebrating small victories, and staying committed to one's craft are the keys to navigating this journey.

The Magic of Belief

Ultimately, the heart of writing fantasy romance lies in the magic of belief—the conviction that within each writer is a world waiting to be discovered, filled with stories of love that transcend boundaries and adventures that stir the soul. Believing in the value of one's voice and the power of the genre to enchant and inspire propels writers forward into the realms of imagination and the pages of their next great love story.

Embarking on the path of a fantasy romance writer is not merely an act of creation but a journey of continuous growth, exploration, and connection. With each story penned, each piece of feedback woven into the fabric of your narrative, and each challenge navigated, you contribute to the ever-expanding universe of fantasy romance. This genre celebrates the boundless potential of love and magic, inviting readers and writers alike to believe in the impossible.

Thank You!

Thanks for making it to the end!

I hope you find this book helpful in your publishing journey.

We ask that you kindly leave a review!

Printed in Great Britain
by Amazon

46543216R00089